Russia
and
Europe

A HISTORY TODAY BOOK

Russia
and
Europe

EDITED BY PAUL DUKES

COLLINS & BROWN

First published in Great Britain in 1991
by Collins & Brown Limited
Mercury House
195 Knightsbridge
London SW7 1RE

The articles in this book were published in
History Today between 1980 and 1990.

A CIP catalogue record for this book
is available from the British Library

ISBN 1 85585 053 2

Typeset by Falcon Graphic Art Ltd, Wallington, Surrey
Printed and bound in Great Britain by The Bath Press, Avon.

Contents

Introduction

PAUL DUKES

Today in the 1990s, as much as ever, discussion of Russia's relationship to Europe remains a high priority for historians and others, both in the academic world and beyond it. In particular, a great debate on this relationship has been taking place on the public platforms of the Soviet Union, and the election of both the first and the last contributor to this series as People's Deputies has been an indication of a widespread desire for scholars to come down from their ivory tower to make their informed comments on such subjects of general interest. At the same time, of course, the relationship between Russia and Europe is one of significance 'for its own sake' (as much as anything can be). As such, its analysis can be developed only through the single-minded endeavours of scholars in Russia and the wider world. And so, whatever representative or administrative functions they may have performed, all our contributors have devoted much of their energies to a range of specialist researches, some of the results of which are now placed before the non-specialist reader, in the best *History Today* manner. In other words, after reading these essays, you should have a better understanding of where the Soviet Union, or its successor/s, may be heading towards the year 2000 and beyond, and whence it, and its predecessors, came a thousand years and more before.

The point of departure is the local variant of the medieval ideal of the universal Church. Adopted from the New Rome, the Byzantine Empire, rather than from the original Rome, whose Pope had given his blessing to the Holy Roman Empire of Charlemagne in the year 800, 'Holy Russia' developed from the reception of Christianity by Prince Vladimir of Kiev in or around the year 988. At the beginning of the sixteenth century, fifty years or so after the fall of Byzantium to the Ottoman Turks, the doctrine of the Third Rome was added to Holy Russia, simultaneously providing a further link with Europe and a reason for remaining apart. This duality is embodied in the evolution of architectural style from Kiev to Muscovy: some Romanesque, almost no Gothic, a distinctive Renaissance and Baroque: and always local variants in these international movements. A further duality was that of the double faith, the admixture of the new Christianity with old Slavic folkways, with at least some observers claiming that Holy Russia was no more than skin deep. Among these were some of the earliest into print, who gave emphasis to the brutality of the people and the tyranny of their princes. And then, the new secularism made its early entry into Russia in the seventeenth century, to be clearly discerned in the reign of Peter the Great's father, Alexis.

But the nature of the father's achievement has long been over-shadowed by that of the son. Few European rulers have enjoyed such fame as has Peter the Great, whose dazzling achievement was to bring secluded Russia into the open society of Europe. Or so it has been asserted over and again, with St Petersburg as solid testimony to the opening of the window on the West. There are limitations to such a view, however, found in distinct echoes of the doctrine of the Third Rome in the secular imperial ideology of Peter's new capital city. The great reformer's achievement must also be seen in a broad perspective embracing the whole continent: in a sense, Russia had not entered modernity before his reign because there was no modernity for it to enter. The very term 'Europe' as distinct from 'Christendom' came into common usage at about the time of Peter's celebrated embassy to the West. We must recognize, too, that this and other grand gestures highlighted the entrance of the man himself as a consummate actor on the world stage, a role which he was to develop throughout the years of the Northern War. On the other hand, Peter the Great cannot be reduced to insignificance, and this collection of essays helps to put him fairly and squarely in his place, from the points of view of international relations, political thought, cultural interaction and personality.

This is not to say that all the contributors agree with each other on every aspect of the relationship of Russia to Europe before, at or after the beginning of the eighteenth century. As always, individual historians have their own outlooks as well as their common commitment to the canons of scholarship. This problem of relativity is well illustrated in the interpretations of a pre-revolutionary Russian, a Ukrainian active before and after the Revolution of 1917, and a Soviet historian of our own age. Today, as several times before but now with a fresh intensity, the question of Russia and Europe is posed along with others about the nature of the constituent parts of the Soviet Union as a whole. Is it possible to draw a single line of development from Kiev through Moscow to St Petersburg and back again to Moscow, or are we obliged to think of many strands, intertwined over the centuries of Russian expansion, but now unravelling themselves? After all, the great debate is not just about the roles of Stalin, Trotsky and Lenin, but also about those of Peter I (the Great), Ivan IV (the Terrible) and Ivan III (the Great).

In the last years of the twentieth century, as throughout the nineteenth and eighteenth and, in different ways, even earlier centuries, there are passionate advocates of the association of Russia with Europe. Others have, with equal conviction, stressed its essential apartness. Other concepts: of 'Holy Russia' and of a materialist alternative to it, have also had their no less committed adherents. The essays in the present collection will make the reader better able to understand the debate, and to participate in it.

CHAPTER I

The Idea of Holy Russia

SERGEI AVERINTSEV

'The most beautiful and peerless capital of all the inhabited earth'. This was how Theodore Metochites, a Byzantine writer, described Constantinople, as late as at the beginning of the fourteenth century. And it was not empty rhetoric.

This was how the Byzantines genuinely felt, and not just they alone. One thousand years before, there had been still more justification for such sentiments than remained in Metochites' time. In the tenth century, the capital on the Bosphorus was undoubtedly, and incomparably, the most splendid city and dazzling centre of culture in the entire Christian world. 'They dreamt of Constantinople among the cold mists of Norway, on the banks of the Russian rivers, in the strong castles of the West and in the counting-houses of avaricious Venice,' as V.L. Lazarev put it in his *History of Byzantine Painting* (1947). Most important of all, this state thought of itself not as the first but as the only one of its kind in the world – and its self-perception was internally quite logical, coherent and convincing. It was without compare, or peerless, as Metochites said. Only three criteria were cited. First, it professed the true, or Orthodox, Christian faith. Second, it managed its state affairs and diplomatic relations in a highly-civilized way that was supplemented by the literary and philosophical culture of classical antiquity. Third, it was the legal successor to the Christian-Imperial Rome of Constantine the Great.

The first criterion totally eliminated oriental competitors: the Asian powers, from the Caliphate to China, were comparable in their statecraft and level of urbanization but they were not Christian. Western competitors were likewise partially eliminated. The final break between the eastern and western churches became a fact of ecclesiastical life in 1054 and of popular awareness by the thirteenth century, especially after the Sack of Constantinople in 1204 by the knights of the Fourth Crusade. However, suspicions about the orthodoxy of western Christianity had grown up in the ninth century when in the 860s Patriarch Photius was already expressing such doubts. The second criterion totally eliminated western competitors. Even Charlemagne's empire at the turn of the ninth century was only a short-lived attempt to reproduce the Roman-Byzantine model with

*Royal sanctity: a fourteenth-century Novgorod icon of Saint Boris
and Saint Gleb – Russian princes seen as holy men in contrast to the
pragmatic traditions of Byzantium.*

an ephemeral conglomeration of unassimilated territories. It also
partially disqualified the oriental competitors: for all their brilliance,
the eastern civilizations did not correspond to the classical standard
and therefore remained barbarian. The third criterion, finally, was in
itself quite sufficient to exclude competition from any other possible
quarter.

However, we must talk separately of the strength of this last
criterion, and its foundations in a particular view of the world.
History itself and then the Christian interpretation of history created

11

a special tie between Rome and Christianity. (Byzantine authors liked to remark that Christ's birth coincided with the reign of the Emperor Augustus.)

The name of the Roman procurator Pontius Pilate became part of the Christian creed, 'for our sake he was crucified under Pontius Pilate'. It is, of course, a rather dismal honour to be remembered as the one who condemned Christ to such a death. Yet even this once again reminded everyone that the secular framework within which the universal sacred history took place was defined by the frontiers of the universal Roman Empire. Only it was of remotely appropriate scale. The tragic irony of the theme of Christ's Passion necessarily presupposes an absolutely serious attitude to authority: the secular authority of Roman law (of which the apostle Paul made special mention), and the sacred authority of the Jewish high priests who destroyed Christ. (In both the Greek and Slavonic texts of the Gospels, and in Byzantine literature and Russian folklore the same word is used for both Orthodox Christian bishops, and Jewish high priests.) 'For there is no power but of God: the powers that be are ordained of God' (Romans 13:1). If it were not so, Golgotha would simply be an unfortunate incident arousing no more than mere pity. The participation of a Roman official and Roman soldiers in the execution of Christ cannot serve as an argument against the appointed mission of Rome in secular history. Their fellow collaborators, the Jews, are the chosen people of the Old Testament. Caiaphas the high priest occupies a position so holy that he is endowed (according to John 11:51) with the ability to prophesy. Judas Iscariot was personally chosen by Christ to be among his twelve disciples. All the *dramatis personae* are chosen. To the Christian mind, Rome is that same world which is under the domination of the 'Prince of this world', i.e. the Devil, but which must be redeemed and sanctified. Having united all the lands of Mediterranean civilization, the Roman Empire in a certain sense actually was *the* world.

For a long time the Roman authorities persecuted the early Christian preachers, but the latter spread through the world along roads made by Roman soldiers. Even at a time when Christians were being thrown to the lions, they believed that the *Pax Romana* was a defensive barrier preventing the coming of the Antichrist. When the Roman Emperor Constantine at last placed the Christian faith under his protection, the experience masterfully defined the medieval outlook as a whole, and for ever shaped that of Byzantium, though it would never again be repeated. The geographical compass within which Roman law was applied, Graeco-Roman culture extended, and the Christian faith freely confessed was one and the same. All of the high intellectual, moral and spiritual values that man knew in the Christian world, both religious and secular, were to be found within the borders of one and the same state: the Bible handed down by the Church, Homer handed down through the schools, Greek philosophy and Roman law. Beyond its confines the world was simultaneously of a different faith ('infidel'), a different culture ('barbarian') and, moreover, so lacking in law and order that it seemed to be not part of the world or the cosmos but chaos, 'outer darkness'. The binary union of the Roman Empire and the Christian Church constituted a world in itself.

This is no mere ideological construct. In the West the empire ceased to exist in 476, but in the East it continued for a further thousand years. Approximately one century after its demise, the learned men of western Europe began rather denigratingly to refer to it as the 'Byzantine' Empire. This title was derived from the classical name for the city on the Bosphorus: it was not the name used in medieval times or by the inhabitants of the Eastern Empire. At the dawn of the Byzantine era, the city had ceased to be Byzantium and became Constantinople or the New Rome. This novel scholarly title instead stressed the gulf separating 'true' antiquity from the 'dark ages' and became widely accepted, at times recovering its original abusive intent (for instance, in nineteenth-century liberal journalism).

The Byzantines never called themselves either Byzantine or Greek. From classical times down to our own day the Greeks have referred to themselves as Hellenes. In Christian usage, however, this word acquired the derogatory meaning of pagans as opposed to Christians. Therefore the inhabitants of the Eastern Empire described themselves as Romans (or *Rhomaioi* in medieval Greek). Considering the uninterrupted continuity of their state, they had every right to this name, and even their enemies could not deny it. When Vitiges, the King of the Ostrogoths, was waging war against Justinian I in the sixth century for control over Italy, he ordered that coins be minted bearing not his own image but that of the emperor. Whoever had real control, the token of authority belonged to the Roman or Romaic emperor. The barbarian young peoples of Europe at odds with Rome, and then with the New Rome, did not think of denying their unique legitimacy. They regarded the empire with profound respect and envy.

With time they made attempts to claim this legitimacy for themselves. On Christmas Day in the year 800 Charlemagne, King of the Franks, was crowned Roman Emperor in Rome by the Bishop of Rome (i.e. the pope). It did not occur to him to proclaim himself emperor, say, of the Franks or the Germans. In Constantinople, of course, the imperial title of Charlemagne and all his successors was regarded as an outrageous usurpation. When the tsars of the Bulgarians and the Serbs began openly to fight against the New Rome, their struggle was nowhere justified by the modern idea of nationalism. They wished to re-create, but now under their own control, that same single and unique state alongside which no other could exist. Perhaps this is why the war against them

*A twelfth-century fresco showing the legendary donation of
Constantine – the supposed conferring of dominion by the Emperor on
Pope Silvester (seen left). This was the basis for the later claims of
western Catholic Christianity to universal imperium.*

was waged with such bitterness: for the Byzantines they were not a
military enemy but impostors and spreaders of sedition. In writing
his treatise on *Monarchy*, Dante would still take it as axiomatic and
indisputable that there should be only one universal Christian state,
and that this should be the Roman Empire.

In the language of early Christianity, retained in both the Orthodox
and Catholic traditions, the Christians are the kin and the people of
God. Their existence as a people was thought of in just as literal and
specific terms as that of the chosen people of the Old Testament; but
this time the chosen people are gathered in from 'every kindred, and
tongue, and people, and nation' (Revelations 5:9) to unite all human-
ity, 'and there shall be one fold and one shepherd'. This idea was taken
seriously. The ethno-cultural antagonisms that flared up from time to
time were perceived and expressed as heresies. The universality of the
Christian Empire, in theory, should correspond to the universality of
the Christian faith just like the caliphate in the Islamic conception. If
in both cases political practice gradually diverged from the theoretical
ideal, that theory retained its rights and continued to pass judgement
on the practice. For medieval man this was an incontrovertible truth.
In Dante we still find a moving condemnation of particularist reality
in terms of the universal doctrine: he quite logically allotted the place
of honour at the beginning of the sixth canto in his *Paradise* to the
Byzantine Emperor Justinian.

Whatever the theories might say, the territory of the Eastern Empire irresistibly contracted. At the end it was almost synonymous with the city of Constantinople, a head too large for its dwarfish body. One needed to be Greek to keep believing that the relation between Constantinople and the rest of the universe, as a Greek saying declared, was of fifteen to a dozen . . . Even in this extreme humiliation, however, the very location of Constantinople on the frontier of Europe and Asia was a token of the Romaic Empire's universalist task. The city did not fit any definition: it was not European but neither was it Asiatic, at least not until the Turks took possession and transformed it into Stamboul. The city that occupies this site is still in some sense a world in itself, just as the Roman Empire was in its day.

Since the Middle Ages, an important concept has found lexical expression in west European, or Christian, languages, which is notably absent both from the Byzantine and traditional, pre-intelligentsia Russian lexicon. In the West it is denoted by the words *christianitas* in medieval Latin, *chrétienté* in French (already used in the *Song of Roland*), *Christenheit* in German, Christendom in English, and so on. In Russian one could only use the later weak and bookish phrase 'the Christian world' (*khristianskii mir*). But it bears no comparison to these other terms in the vitality or necessity of its existence. What they denote is the totality of all Christian countries and nations in relation to which each of them individually is only a subordinate part. This was how western Europe referred to itself before it began to use the terms West or Europe. (We may compare the title of one of the philosophical works by the German Romantic author, Novalis, *Die Christenheit oder Europa*, where the two words are linked and equated.) No matter what enmities might divide the territories, cities and kingdoms of Europe – and in the modern period, its nations as well – and no matter how far the self-assertion of each of its parts might reach, they remained subordinate to the whole, to a self-evident and objective order. In fact it was this rivalry, competition and mutual restraint that established the natural frontiers of each and maintained its status as part of the whole. As the guarantee of their higher unity, the medieval world-view placed two figures over and above these parts, the emperor and the pope. Yet it was just because each of these active political forces could only be a part and were not entitled to represent the whole, that the empire could not be set up in the West.

Let us return, however, to the western words we have just mentioned. As was said, there is no logical equivalent to them in the pre-modern Russian language. Perhaps there is, nevertheless, a functional equivalent. Their functional purpose was to give earthly expression to the theological concept of the universal Church and place it in a more carnal and, at the same time, epic perspective.

It was to be, we might say, a historiosophic perspective for use by the layman. In the Russian popular vocabulary this function was performed by the phrase 'Holy Russia' (and, correspondingly, the 'Holy Russian land'). It is important to grasp that this concept in no way refers to what we now call the national idea, or to geographical and ethnic criteria. Holy Russia is an almost cosmic category. At least, within its limits (or its limitless extent!) both the Eden of the Old Testament and the Palestine of the gospels have their place. G.P. Fedotov in his time collected eloquent illustrations of this idea in his study of Russian spiritual folklore:

> A beautiful sun lit up in Paradise,
> King Herod sent his messengers
> throughout the Holy Russian land.
> The Virgin walked through Holy Russia.
> She was seeking for her Son . . .

It would be unbearably limited to understand this as an expression of tribal *folie de grandeur*. It is, moreover, the entire point of this term that no ethnic reference is involved here. What then are we to make of this? Is it a need to bring the sacred figures and events closer? Hardly. Such a desire is incomparably more typical of west European Christianity, at least from the late Middle Ages onwards. For, on the contrary, a Russian generally regards a familiar intimacy with the sacred as blasphemous, and prefers the austere feeling of separation. No Russian saint would have thought of making a Christmas crèche as Francis of Assisi did in Greccio, thereby for ever establishing one of the most widely practised customs among Catholic nations. We may also consider certain other examples. In verse, William Blake summed up the experience of Protestant sectarian spirituality in the arbitrary context of proto-Romanticism when he expressed the intention to build 'Jerusalem in England's green and pleasant land'. The Catholic Middle Ages also, incidentally, had their Jerusalems: churches laid out according to the disposition of the holy places in Jerusalem (the abbey of Santo-Stefano in Bologna with its many chapels is one example). When Patriarch Nikon wanted to build a New Jerusalem in Russia in the seventeenth century, however, his detractors regarded this as dishonouring a sacred place: 'Is it good that the name of the Holy City should be thus transferred, given to another place and disgraced?' A century after Blake, another English poet, the Catholic Francis Thompson, talked of Christ walking on the waters 'not of Gennesaret but Thames'. This mention of the Thames leads us by contrast to note that although the events in Russian spiritual verse were repeatedly said to take place in Holy Russia it was inconceivable that any Russian river might be referred to there. They speak of Jordan but not of Russian rivers. (The same Patriarch Nikon renamed the River Istra, Jordan. Setting aside for a

*T*he claim of western Catholic Christianity to universal imperium
was shared by the Pope and the Holy Roman Emperor, reflected in the
drawing above of the coronation of Frederick III by Pope Nicholas V
in Rome in 1452.

moment the Russian view that this was a dangerous impertinence
there was, even here, no familiarity with the River Jordan. Rather
it was a purifying and thus a distancing and alienation of the River
Istra itself.)

We have to wait for the nineteenth century, i.e. for a culture
with quite different foundations, before a poet like Tiutchev could
see Holy Russia as a truly Russian landscape. Only then was the
land to which he imagined the King of Heaven coming as a
pauper in his poem geographically and ethnically identified with
Russia: 'These poor settlements, this austere landscape . . .' The
landscape of Holy Russia in the early spiritual verses is different.
When they began to build the church of Zion there, they indeed

17

used quintessentially Russian trees, birch and rowan. Yet the most important wood of all was the southern, Mediterranean cypress of the Imperial City and Jerusalem, although most Russians were more familiar with its scent from the crucifixes brought back by pilgrims than with its natural appearance. So there are birches and rowan trees, but the cypress is, nevertheless, more important than either. The Romantic imagination vainly sought for local colour. There are no identifiably local features in Holy Russia. It has only two features: first, that it is in some sense the whole world and even encompasses paradise; second, that it is the world under the sign of the true religion. In the well-known early Russian poem about the *Golubinaya Kniga*, the only justification for the White, i.e. Russian, tsar's prerogative is that he is a Christian king. Since it happens that there are no other Christian rulers in the whole world, however, his rights become exceptionally far-reaching:

> Our White king is king over kings.
> Why is the White king, king over kings?
> He accepted the baptismal faith,
> the baptismal, the orthodox faith.
> And he believes in the indivisible Trinity . . .

It is important who instructed the Russians in matters of faith. Their teachers were the Orthodox Byzantines who insisted, for the sake of asserting their own authority, that Church and empire were quite inseparable. In this respect, the admonition administered to Vasily I, the Prince of Moscow, by Patriarch Antony IV of Constantinople was typical. The former had dared to proclaim that the Russians shared a Church with the Byzantines but did not have an emperor, i.e. for them the Byzantine monarch, who was for the time being the only Orthodox emperor, was not their king. 'It is impossible for Christians to have a Church and not to have an Empire', noted the Patriarch. 'For Church and Empire form a great union and it is impossible for them to be separated.' Historically speaking, it is highly significant that these words were addressed by a spiritual leader to a secular lord, and by a Byzantine to the Prince of Moscow in the 1390s. The Byzantine Empire would continue to exist for little more than half a century: soon after its fall the Prince's descendants would lay the foundations of the Russian Empire. If no less a figure than the patriarch of the imperial city so authoritatively explained to the ruler of Moscow that the Orthodox Empire was the essential concomitant and in some way the full expression of the Orthodox Church, how could he not take such a lesson to heart, once and for all time?

It is further important that the rise of Moscow coincided chronologically with the fall of Constantinople. In 1453, the Turks entered the capital on the Bosphorus, and in 1461 they took possession of Trebizond, the last fragment of the Romaic Empire. In 1478

Moscow annexed the territory of Novgorod and in 1480 finally threw off the Mongol-Tartar yoke. The idea of a Third Rome as an alternative to Constantinople is well known from the letter written by the Pskov *starets*, or elder, Filofei (Philotheus) in the sixteenth century: '. . . two Romes have fallen, the third stands, and a fourth there shall not be . . .' Yet this formula was not new, it had been developed earlier in southern Slavic writings. Recalling the collapse of the Western Empire in 476, a Byzantine chronicler concluded: 'So that is what happened to the old Rome, but our Rome flourishes, grows, rules and is rejuvenated.' In a fourteenth-century Bulgarian translation, however, these words were significantly altered: '. . . and that having happened to the old Rome, our own new imperial city grows, and becomes stronger and younger'. Judging by all else, the new imperial city (Tsargrad) was Tyrnovo, the capital of the Bulgarian empire. Consequently, where the Byzantine chronicler addressed the emperor was inserted an address to Ioann Alexander, the Bulgarian tsar, 'great lord and fair conqueror'. This is a very stable logical structure. Rome has fallen but we are unconquered, and we are Rome. In this the Byzantine chronicler, his Bulgarian translator, and the Russian Filofei are all thoroughly at one.

After this, however, their historical destinies diverge. The southern Slavic kingdoms rebelled when Constantinople was still standing. They were forced to engage in an unseemly dispute with her over their claim to be the one and only Orthodox power, and they succumbed to the Turks in the late thirteenth century, even before the end of Byzantium itself. The principality of Muscovy, quite to the contrary, had hardly emerged when it immediately found itself beyond any dispute the only Orthodox state in the world and not within the reach of Islam. There was a new configuration of historical circumstances that for centuries made Filofei's words true in the most literal sense. Or perhaps it was not an entirely novel situation, after all? The inimitable period of Constantine's reign seemed to be repeating itself. Once again there was only one state that embodied the true faith on earth and, unlike the western Catholic states, it could not be compared to or enter into any relations of subordination with its other fellow-Christian states. When the common people talked in one of the spiritual verses about the White king's authority 'over all lands, over the universe', the meaning was not political, it meant something more than that.

Alongside the confessional definition, the geographical aspect is also important. Kievan Russia was territorially large, but as a state was contained within certain self-evident limits: it could still feel itself an integral, if marginal, part of the whole – of European *Christianitas*. Confessional differences were still not so acutely felt that they could obstruct dynastic marriages, for instance, between the ruling houses of Russia and the West. After the Tartar conquest, however, and especially after Ivan III had freed Russia again and Ivan IV (the Terrible) had triumphantly campaigned against the Tartars, Russia increasingly became a Eurasian entity; after the khanates of Kazan and Astrakhan had been conquered, Moscow became no less of a Eurasian power than Byzantium, though in a different way. Each of these stages corresponded to an ever more conscious alienation of Russia from the Catholic West: in the thirteenth century Alexander Nevsky rejected the pope's envoy; in the fifteenth century Prince Vasily II dethroned the Latinophile Greek Metropolitan of Moscow, Isidore; and under Ivan the Terrible the mission of Antonio Possevino met with failure. Now the Russians no longer simply followed after their Greek masters but, on the contrary, saw the reason for the downfall of Byzantium and their own appointed mission as lying in the compromise the Greeks had made with the Latin Church. Russia was also a world in itself.

It is appropriate to recall here the last phrase of Chaadaev's uncompleted 'Apology of a Madman' where he referred to the 'geographical fact' that 'imperiously dominates our historical evolution'. The competitive mutual balance between the forces that strive to expand and thereby restrain each other was highly typical of European history, but can only be observed on Russia's western borders. Three long centuries were needed just to resolve the rivalry between Moscow and Lithuania. As a result, it was Petersburg that shared in the partitions of Poland, but the western drive towards medieval Russia was never as irresistible as that of the Mongol-Tartars. On the western borders, the picture could only change slowly, but in other directions Russia seemed to be almost entirely without natural frontiers. During the reign of Ivan the Terrible, Russian territory was expanded eastwards to the Irtysh river and beyond. A west European state could only make a similar expansion at the expense of territories overseas – but that was already quite a different matter, both objectively and psychologically. In the Russian case it was not simply the annexation of territory beyond Europe by a European power, but the creation of a united Eurasian arena, not for the Russian people but for the Orthodox faith. Holy Russia, I repeat, was not an ethnic concept. The legend of Pyotr or Peter, son of the king of the Golden Horde, provided deliberate illustration of this: when Russia is still under the Mongol yoke, a young Tartar of the royal blood adopts the Orthodox faith, builds a church in Rostov, and charms the Russians with his 'sweet responses'. The Byzantine epos (epic poem) of Digenes Acritas offers a comparable, though much less religion-imbued plot. Digenes' father is a noble Arab emir who is baptized and thereby becomes a member of the Byzantine nobility, but he does so rather out of love for his Byzantine betrothed, it must be admitted, than for any more spiritual motives. Both the Romaic and the Muscovite state are open to those who will accept their faith. The reverse side of such universalism was the weakly developed theme of the natural tie linking an ethnic group to its state. In both these cases, the link was founded not on natural so much as supernatural foundations. And to speak simply and bluntly, the position of a converted Tartar in the reign of Ivan the Terrible was much better than that of indigenous Russians from Novgorod, say. However, the Byzantine Greeks also sacrificed their own ethnic name when they replaced it with one accepted from the alien hands of universal statehood.

All these are features of deep similarity between the religious understanding of statehood in Byzantium and in Russia. However, we cannot help noting that there was also an important difference. The Byzantine monarchical system was inherited from the Roman Empire. This had two vital consequences.

First, the Roman Empire was directly descended from the system of personal rule of successful military leaders like Sulla and Caesar, which had matured in a very civilized age after centuries of republican government. It did not emerge from the archaic patriarchal order.

The affirmation of Russian nationhood: a celebration of Alexander Nevsky Day at the Nevsky Monastery in St Petersburg in September 1906.

Short-lived dynasties might come and go, but the dynastic principle as a fact of moral awareness was lacking. Also very weak was the idea of the individual's duty of loyalty to the emperor's person: in both Rome and Byzantium, the monarchs were easily overthrown and put to death, sometimes publicly and with the participation of the gloating mob. This does not mean that nothing was sacred for the Byzantine. The most sacred thing on earth for him was the empire itself which, as we have seen, embraced a self-sufficient plenitude of politico-juridical, cultural and religious values. Therefore, incidentally, such a figure as the Russian Prince Kurbsky would hardly be possible in Byzantium. (Fearing disgrace because of his closeness to the feudal lords executed by Ivan the Terrible, the nobleman Kurbsky fled to Lithuania.) A Byzantine fugitive seemed, by contrast, to pass out of existence when he fled to the barbarians and no one would have listened to him or begun to denounce him as the Russians did in regard to the renegade Kurbsky. The empire was indeed very sacred, as was the office of emperor: however, the most capable and successful should wear the imperial regalia and, if it happened to be a usurper, that only made his ability and success more conspicuous. (The successes of the leader, military commander and politician were not perceived as the result of favourable circumstances, but as an immanent quality of their personality, or secular 'charisma'. Cicero had even seriously discussed such an idea.) The impostors and false Dmitrys, who were so characteristic of the medieval and then the modern Russian autocracy, were not typical of the history of the Byzantine autocracy. Why go to the trouble of adopting another's name when success was in itself sufficient to justify any usurpation?

Whatever might be spiritually required in the way of purely private repentance, the Byzantine thought that in politics God was for the winner (unless, of course, the winner was a heretic). The Byzantine was true to his empire until the last, but loyalty to the ruler endured only so long as he was convinced that the individual concerned pragmatically corresponded to the majesty of the empire. The murder of the ruler, at times by the people, is described again and again with dispassionate openness in Byzantine historical works. It is one of those unhappy but unimportant events that are necessarily presupposed by the very existence of politics, they imply. Such unfortunate events do not notably weigh on the popular conscience. A Byzantine would not have understood the lament of the Patriarch Pimen in Pushkin's *Boris Godunov*, and yet the poet here captured a major theme of traditional Russian psychology:

> We have angered God, we have sinned:
> As our lord and master we have proclaimed a regicide.

In the middle of the civilized nineteenth century, a legend arose in Russia about the holy elder Fyodor Kuzmich – ordinary Russians could not tolerate the thought that Alexander I should have died on the throne when he had been involved in the killing of his father, Paul I. The Byzantine, in turn, would not have understood how Boris and Gleb (and later the tsarevich Dmitry) could be numbered among the saints. They did not die for their faith, after all, but were merely the victims of the mundane order of things. Everyone knows that the world is steeped in wickedness and there are a great many blameless victims on earth! There are martyrs among the Russian saints, those who died for their beliefs; but just try to ask even a very well-read and devout Christian about them. No one recalls Prince Roman Olgovich of Ryazan, who was cut to pieces by the Tartars of the Golden Horde for blaspheming against their deity; or Kukshu, who was missionary to the natives of Vyatka in the Urals; and our informant will only recall Mikhail of Chernigov with some difficulty. However, for centuries all have remembered Boris and Gleb and the young tsarevich stabbed to death in Uglich. It turns out that it is only in this 'long-suffering' endurance of hardship, without any act or even a martyr's 'testimony' of faith, but merely 'accepting' one's bitter cup, that the holiness of the imperial dignity is truly embodied. Only by their suffering is the existence of the empire justified. To explain why this is so demands thorough and unhurried reflection.

Meanwhile we may note a simple historical fact. It was important that the Russian princes constituted a single lineage, while the throne in Constantinople was open to any adventurer, no matter where he came from. It was also important that monarchy in Russia did not grow up as a pragmatic solution, but developed out of patriarchal relations. Finally, there is the contrast between Byzantine rationality and the Russian state of mind.

Furthermore, the circumstances by which Christian Byzantium received its political system from pagan Rome did not give the Christian consciousness of the Romaics the opportunity to experience autocracy as a problem. (Moreover, the final shape was given to this system by the last 'persecutor' of Christianity, Diocletian.) For the Byzantines autocracy was not a problem; it was part of the nature of things. In Russia everything took a rather different path.

CHAPTER II

The West comes to Russian Architecture

LINDSEY HUGHES

Western architecture is generally believed to have come to Russia with the foundation of St Petersburg in 1703, Peter the Great's 'Window on the West'. Cultural historians have made effective use of the contrast between 'wooden' Moscow, decidedly Russian, even 'oriental' in its picturesque disorder, and 'stone' St Petersburg, the regular and rational product of the European Enlightenment. The truth, as with many such handy formulae, is more complex. Tourists who take Moscow's Red Square as their starting point, approaching it from Marx Prospekt, may initially be arrested by the exotic silhouette of sixteenth-century St Basil's Cathedral, but if they look to the right they will see the red-brick walls of the Kremlin, constructed by Italians in the 1480s–90s, and the Spassky Tower, its upper portion designed by an Englishman in the 1620s. Even St Basil's has a surprisingly regular, almost 'Classical' ground plan. The fact is, Russian art has never been totally isolated from outside influences, even though until the end of the seventeenth century it displayed a much more limited range of genres and conventions than the art of most west European countries.

The event that largely determined the forms of national art for the next 700 years was the reception of Christianity from Byzantium around 988. Conversion brought Russia the Eastern Orthodox brand of faith, art, architecture and literacy, but, as Dmitry Obolensky has pointed out, 'Byzantium was not a wall erected between Russia and the West. She was Russia's gateway to Europe.' As anyone familiar with the art of twelfth-century Sicily or St Mark's in Venice will know, Byzantine culture was by no means limited to the 'East'. In Russia's case, it provided an essential link with classical antiquity. In addition, Kievan Russia, far from being cut off from Europe, maintained close contact with its major courts. Grand Prince Yaroslav the Wise (1019–54) was himself married to a Swede and gave his daughters in marriage to the Kings of France, Hungary and Norway. His major foundation, the Cathedral of the Holy Wisdom in Kiev (*circa* 1037), emulated Justinian's Sancta Sophia in Constantinople, the most magnificent example of a domed church in East or West. It combined standard Byzantine inscribed cross and Greek constructional techniques with thirteen cupolas, a reflection of

*St Basil's Cathedral, Moscow, completed in 1561 is the best-known
example of a 'tent' church, but with Renaissance elements. To the
right is the Spassky Tower of the Kremlin.*

the Russian love of a picturesque skyline. From the outset, foreign
models were adapted to local climate, materials and tastes.

Contact between Russia and Europe at this time is evident,
not so much in Kiev itself, but in other principalities. In the
city of Chernigov, for example, there are churches decorated with
an arcading frieze and half-columns with capitals characteristic of
Romanesque art. Further west, in the Galicia-Volhynia or Grodno
areas, one sees even more markedly western features in what was
effectively a cultural crossroads.

The strongest echoes of Romanesque are found in the north-east,
where in the twelfth century the principality of Vladimir-Suzdal laid
claim to political predominance. The elegant white stone churches
have long both impressed and puzzled with their friezes of blind
arcading, recessed portals, carved columns and relief sculpture. The
rounded bays and arches of the Cathedral of the Assumption in Vladimir (1158–61) are reminiscent of the articulation of Romanesque
architecture, although the five domes over an inscribed cross are, of
course, Byzantine. The chronicle records that God brought masters
to the builder, Prince Andrei Bogolyubsky, 'from all lands', but there
is no precise evidence of sources. Visual evidence may suggest many
possible influences – Armenian, Georgian, Galician, Italian, German –

but the Assumption Cathedral and its contemporaries, the Church of the Intercession on the Nerl (1165) and the Cathedral of St Demetrius (1194) are probably best viewed as further developments on Russian soil of Orthodox conventions, the forms of which were receptive to Romanesque devices.

It should be noted in passing that the usual material for all structures was, and remained, wood. Brick and stone and the comparatively few masters qualified to work them were almost exclusively reserved for ecclesiastical buildings, which gives a peculiar slant to the study of Russian architectural history today, as the buildings where people lived and worked have largely disappeared. The fact that the surviving buildings, mainly churches, followed a different set of conventions from those of the Catholic and Protestant West meant that there was to be no wholesale borrowing of western models. As long as Church and State honoured the conventions, 'westernization' would occur on a limited scale.

The independence and prosperity of Kievan Russia was brought to an end by the Mongol invasion of 1237–40. Some areas escaped the full onslaught, however, and were able to resume architectural activities fairly quickly.

The most notable was the city-state of Novgorod which was able to maintain trade relations with Scandinavia and Germany as a member of the Hanseatic League. Foreign merchants lived there and even built their churches in the city, but for all its contacts Novgorod architecture in the thirteenth and fourteenth centuries remained strongly independent. At a time when western neighbours were elaborating the complex forms of the Gothic, the designs of Novgorod churches show a tendency towards simplification and the articulation of all elements into an austere whole, built without the aid of precise measurements or plans. Yet, even in this distinctive style, one cannot escape from hints of the architecture of neighbouring countries. Baltic features may be detected in the design of portals and windows, in two-tiered arcades on apses or the vertical division of façades. In particular, the stepped rooflines seem to have counterparts in much north European domestic architecture, but it is impossible to specify paths of diffusion. Only in the case of a rib-vaulted chamber commissioned by Archbishop Euphymius in 1433 do we learn that it was, indeed, constructed with the help of 'Germans from across the sea'.

The Mongols themselves exerted no direct influences on Russian architecture, in Novgorod or elsewhere. On the contrary, by allowing the Orthodox Church autonomy and exemption from taxes, they indirectly encouraged the continuity of artistic traditions, doubly cherished under foreign domination. The major impact of the Mongols may have been in insulating Russia from the Gothic – the only major European style to make virtually no inroads there. As it was,

Gothic architecture stopped just short of Russia's western borders, in Lithuania and Belorussia, where its presence may be explained by the freer movement of artists and the influence of the Catholic Church. In Russia, as Novgorod shows, even where paths of diffusion were open, impact was slight. It may be that Russian builders did not possess the required skills, that there were no funds available for Gothic cathedrals on the grand scale and, most important, that the forms of Gothic were too out of keeping with Orthodox conventions to be easily assimilated. By the time Russia looked to the West for architects, the West itself had entered an artistic era with more easily adaptable forms.

By the fifteenth century, the power of the Mongols was in decline and Russia was on the verge of unification under the leadership of Moscow and its Grand Prince Ivan III or 'the Great' (1462–1505), 'gatherer of the Russian lands'. It is natural that Ivan should have wished to embellish Moscow's citadel, the Kremlin, as the centre of his new realm, but the approach he took was determined by his marriage in 1472 to Zoë Palaeologue, niece of the last Emperor of Byzantium. Zoë had been educated in Rome as a ward of the Pope and thus provided a link with the mainstream of contemporary European art. The Renaissance thus came remarkably early to Russia.

In 1475, the architect Aristotele Fioravanti of Bologna (*circa* 1415–85/6) came to Moscow to construct a cathedral dedicated to the Assumption of the Virgin as a mother church for all Russia, a version attempted by Russian builders having collapsed shortly before his arrival. This contemporary of Bramante and Alberti was not to be allowed simply to transplant some Renaissance design from Catholic soil, however. His model was to be the twelfth-century Cathedral of the Assumption in Vladimir, as an indication of both the status of Orthodox conventions and the dynastic link of the Muscovite princes with Kievan Russia. The church he built (1475–9) reproduces the semi-circular bays and five domes of the original (and, incidentally, an echo of Romanesque in the blind arcading), but the symmetry and engineering were of the Renaissance, for example in the proportions of the four bays of the south façade or in the neat solution of the apses.

Fioravanti introduced Russians to new types of brickwork and foundations and the use of iron supports. His cathedral was copied all over Russia. Just before his death, Ivan III also commissioned a mausoleum. The resulting Cathedral of the Archangel Michael (1505–9) was designed by the Italian Alevisio Novy ('the New') and adheres faithfully to the five-domed convention, but its decoration was to set trends for the next two centuries: walls deceptively articulated into two storeys, cornices, pilasters and Venetian-style semi-circular shell gables.

The Italians did much else to transform the centre of Moscow. In 1487–91 Pietro Solari and Marco Friazin (Ruffo) built the palazzo-style Faceted Chamber, and from 1485 Solari and his team

The 'wooden city' of Moscow in the seventeenth century. Almost all secular buildings were made of wood; only ecclesiastical buildings used the more permanent, and expensive, brick or stone.

erected the walls of the Kremlin with their swallowtail battlements. Yet, simultaneously, a church was constructed which bore witness to the tenacity of native traditions. The Kremlin Cathedral of the Annunciation (1484–9) was built by craftsmen from Pskov, a town which, like Novgorod, had escaped the worst of the Mongols. In it they combined vaulting constructions from their own region with *kokoshnik* (ogee) gables, soon to be the hallmark of Muscovite architecture, and some token blind arcading from the Vladimir period. 'westernization' still had a long way to go.

In fact, just three decades after the completion of the Italianate Archangel Cathedral, church architecture set off in new native directions. The Church of the Ascension at Kolomenskoe, built by order of Vasily III in 1532, daringly abandoned Byzantine conventions in favour of a pyramidal tower, which at first glance looks Gothic in inspiration. The walls, however, are utterly solid and monumental, the shape derived from Russian timber churches, which had long used octagonal or 'tent' towers. One Soviet writer has described the church as a kind of 'gesture' to the outside world, 'an upsurge of national consciousness, reflecting the strength and pride of a nation which had thrown off the yoke of foreign domination'. It should be noted, however, that some of the detailing hints at Italian influence.

The more famous successor of the Church of the Ascension is the Cathedral of St Basil the Blessed (formerly of the Intercession) on Red Square, built by Ivan the Terrible in 1555–61 to commemorate Russia's victory over the Khanate of Kazan. It seems perverse now that St Basil's was once attributed to an Italian architect or traced to Hindu architecture. It belongs quite clearly to the category of 'tent' (*shatyor*) churches inspired by wooden prototypes, whilst its decoration can be traced not only to woodcarving but also to the *kokoshniki* of brick architecture and even to certain features of the Renaissance repertoire. Renaissance thinking, too, may be detected in the ingenious grouping of nine towers in the ground plan.

Just two years before the construction of this most Russian of buildings, Muscovy had seen an irreversible widening of contacts with the West, when the ship *Bonaventure* captained by Richard Chancellor docked on the White Sea coast. In 1564 the first book was printed in Muscovy. Horizons were opening which were eventually to affect architecture. After the death of Ivan the Terrible's only surviving son in 1598, Russia plunged into the 'Time of Troubles' with dynastic crisis, peasant war, famine and foreign invasion. The arrival of Swedes and Poles, the latter occupying Moscow from 1610–12, exerted little direct cultural influence, but the disaster gave rise to the policy of 'using the West to beat the West', adopted so effectively by Peter I. The reigns of the first Romanovs Mikhail (1613–45) and Alexis (1645–76) saw the hiring of foreigners on a large scale.

The arrival of mercenaries, experts on explosives, weapons and fortification, merchants and craftsmen opened the way for the more direct assimilation of things western, including architecture. It was during Mikhail's reign, for example, that Christopher Galloway built the upper portion of the Kremlin Spassky Tower, installing a clock. The names of many foreign builders appear in official records, for example John Taller, 'master of palace building', who carried out restoration work in the Kremlin, and Johann Kristler from Sweden, who designed a never completed bridge over the Moskva river.

In 1652 an area of Moscow was set aside for foreigners. This was a Church-inspired attempt to isolate 'Latins' and 'Germans' from the populace, but it resulted in a thriving 'corner of western Europe', where, in the words of a Polish observer in 1678, everything was 'neat and orderly as it is in German towns'. There is little direct evidence of the influence of the 'German quarter', as it was known, on the development of Russian architecture, but the glimpses of the West that it afforded may have helped to promote changes in Russian taste for accoutrements such as foreign furniture, mirrors and fabrics.

In the second half of the seventeenth century secular painting, hitherto frowned upon by the Church, made its appearance. Even icon-painting was invaded by perspective and naturalism.

An interesting example of new trends in Russian art is provided by the Church of the Trinity in Nikitniki (1631–53), built not far from Red Square for a wealthy merchant. At heart it bears witness to the continuity of old traditions, with its central cube capped by five cupolas; yet the four side cupolas and drums are solid brick, mere tokens of Byzantine forms. The architect's imaginative flair was expended on picturesque annexes, including a bell-tower and porch surmounted by the favourite 'tent', and on decorative details. Amongst Russian *kokoshniki* lurk elements of the Classical Order system, for example recessed half-columns and classically profiled pediments on the south façade. Here is eloquent evidence that the West had indeed arrived in Russia in the seventeenth century. Similar echoes of the Order system are found in many buildings of the period, including the Kremlin Terem Palace (1635–6) where Classical pediments are set alongside Russian motifs.

Innovations in culture did not go unchallenged. In the 1650s Patriarch Nikon, alongside his attempt to return the rituals and texts of the Orthodox Church to original Greek practice, also 'corrected' architectural forms. His own Kremlin Cathedral of the Twelve Apostles (1655–8) turned back the clock to the style of twelfth-century Vladimir. Yet Nikon and other conservatives also contributed to new trends. At the same time as he banned the 'tent' roof as a departure from Byzantine practice, he started to build a monastery outside Moscow with a cathedral church in imitation of the Church of the Holy Sepulchre in Jerusalem. It had the largest 'tent' roof ever seen in Russia, was constructed on the basis of architectural drawings (not yet commonly in use) and its decoration was executed by a team of craftsmen from Belorussia, who introduced further elements of the Order system into the Russian repertoire.

Members of the Belorussian team were transferred to royal projects in Moscow after Nikon's downfall and their individual style of wood-carving and ceramics made an important contribution to the introduction of western motifs. 'Polish' style had official approval. When Tsar Alexis was fighting the heretical 'Latins' in the Polish war of 1654–67 he took the opportunity to inspect towns such as Vilna, Polotsk and Vitebsk. In the words of his English physician Samuel Collins: 'Since His Majesty has been in Poland and seen the manner of the Princes' houses there and ghess'd at the mode of their Kings, his thoughts are advanc'd and he begins to model his court and edifices more statley . . .'

Western devices were thus assimilated initially through the court, especially through the royal workshops such as the Armoury (*Oruzheinaya palata*), which had illustrated materials at their disposal. Alexis himself owned a book illustrating 'the stone buildings of all German states', and works by Vignola, Serlio, Palladio, Dieterlin and other theoreticians of the Renaissance and Baroque eras, as well as illustrated works on non-architectural topics, were available to Russian craftsmen. One may see their influence in precise architectural elements in the works of the court icon painter, Simon Ushakov, who had never set foot outside Muscovy.

The culmination of these diverse yet undirected influences comes in the 1680s with the arrival of the so-called 'Moscow Baroque' style. Some of the earliest examples are reminiscent of the church in Nikitniki in their general shape and colouration, but their architects had evidently assimilated a new sense of symmetry and regularity in their ordering of both structural and decorative elements. Old Russian devices are now replaced entirely by western details – half-columns with pediments and bases, window surrounds of broken pediments, volutes, carved columns and shell gable motifs. Terms like *baza* (base) and *karniz* (cornice) enter the Russian vocabulary. A further development of Moscow Baroque were tower churches composed of a cubic base supporting a tier of receding octagons, surrounded by annexes and decorated with a range of western-inspired motifs. The churches at Fili (1693–4), Troitse-Lykovo (1698–1704) and Ubory (1694–7) all owe something to distant prototypes in Russian wooden architecture, but the new sense of harmony in their design and planning harks back to the era of the Renaissance.

Ivan III's mausoleum, the Cathedral of Archangel Michael, was designed by Alevisio Novy with the pronounced Venetian elements in the decoration.

Moscow Baroque has been described as the most consistently western style to appear in Russia before 'westernization' became a matter of official policy. Yet no Moscow Baroque building, with the exception of some Ukrainian designs, can be traced back to a foreign prototype. Even the most extreme manifestation of the style, the Church of the Sign at Dubrovitsy (1690–1704), for all its Latin inscriptions, free-standing sculptures and 'crown' cupola, is still recognizably a Russian 'tent' church and closely related to the churches at Fili and Ubory. One is not surprised to hear that there is scant evidence of foreign architects in Russia during the 1680s–90s. On the contrary, some of the best examples of Moscow Baroque have been attributed to Russian architects.

The real coming of the West to Russian architecture is associated with the reign of Peter the Great, who came to the throne at the age of nine in 1682. He grew up with Moscow Baroque, but had no influence upon it. His own remodelling of his country and subjects is often epitomized by his decision to cut off his nobles' beards and order them to don western dress, but in the end it was perhaps his remodelling of Russian architecture that did most to change Russia's image.

These changes are most usually associated with the founding of a new city and the possibilities it offered for a clean sheet for planning and design, but 'Petrine' trends were well under way before the founding of St Petersburg in 1703. The 1680s had already seen an upsurge in the building of brick and stone residences in Moscow, liberally embellished with Moscow Baroque motifs, and the 1690s saw the construction of large-scale public buildings like the Sukharev Tower (1692–1701) (the seat of the first School of Mathematics and Navigation), the Pharmacy or *zemskii prikaz* (late 1690s) and the Mint (1697). Peter marked his victory over the Turks at Azov in 1696 with the construction of triumphal arches, and whereas in his father's day craftsmen in the Armoury had mostly expended their energies on religious objects, under Peter they turned their attention more and more to banners, battle scenes and engravings. Foreigners such as Mario Fontana and Ivan Zarudny were hired for major projects.

Russia was obviously making the transition towards secular art before 1703, but a 'natural' process of assimilation was to prove too slow for Peter's purposes. In 1697–8, during the Grand Embassy to Europe, his eye was attuned to western style in a way that would have been impossible had he remained in Russia; then, in 1703, he was faced with a demand for architects and craftsmen that could not be met from native resources. The solution was to hire foreigners on an unprecedented scale. Those who worked in Russia from 1703 included Andreas Schlüter, Georg Johann Mattarnovy, Gottfried Schädel, Jean-Baptiste Le Blond, Nicolo Michetti and, the most prolific, Domenico Trezzini whose works include the Summer Palace,

*The Church of the Transfiguration, Novodevichy Convent, 1688,
a blend of Muscovite and classical architecture.*

the Twelve Colleges, the Alexander Nevsky Monastery and, most striking of all, the Cathedral of the Peter-Paul Fortress (1712–33), the burial place of the Russian emperors and empresses. The cathedral, with its tall spire and basilical plan, broke with Orthodox conventions in the manner of Protestant northern Europe. Trezzini also worked as Master of Building, Construction and Fortification, supplying, amongst other things, plans for city residences, the proportions of which were determined by the rank of their owners. Uniformity of materials and decoration, regular rooflines and straight vistas were imposed with the aim of achieving that brand of 'Utopian rationalism' so clearly absent in Moscow, whilst the city's role as naval base and trading centre injected a secular atmosphere lacking in the old capital.

The Trezzini period of Petersburg architecture reflected Peter's own preference for the Low Countries. In 1724 he wrote:

> I myself was in France, where they allow of no ornamentation in architecture and build everything flat and simple and solid – all from stone and not brick. I have heard something of Italy from three Russians who have studied there and know the country. But in neither of these places is the architecture suited to our own situation – the most suitable is the Dutch.

It should be noted, however, that the by no means consistent 'Dutch' style of early St Petersburg was achieved by non-Dutch architects who had worked in northern Europe. Peter himself succumbed to the French style when he visited Paris in 1717 and set about embellishing Peterhof, his own version of Versailles, with the help of the architect Le Blond. There was nothing purist or even consistent about Peter's translation of western art forms to Russian soil. What was required was a generally European effect and, when the real article was not to hand, as for example in a shortage of stone for domestic buildings, wooden exteriors were painted in imitation of masonry.

Peter's reforms were ultimately aimed at developing *Russian* skills and to this end he laid the foundations of a school of native architects who would be fully conversant with the Classical idiom and the most up-to-date technology. Foreigners like Trezzini were ordered to set up training facilities on construction sites. In 1709 the Chancellery of Building was established and in the same year the first Russian architectural book, a version of Vignola's *Rules of the Five Orders of Architecture*, was published. It was used as a manual by trainee builders and supplemented by works printed in Europe. Peter's own library contained over 100 titles on architecture and allied crafts.

As early as 1696 Peter had sent a group of nobles abroad to study navigation, and this was to become the practice for certain architects, too. Several of the generation who began work in the 1730s – Ivan Korobov, Ivan Michurin, Peter Eropkin – had studied their craft in Holland or Italy. As skills scarcely known in Russia

a generation before – mathematics, geometry, foreign languages –
were acquired, so a new type of expert emerged who was able, both
technically and psychologically, to work in the foreign idiom. In turn,
their buildings provided an appropriate backdrop for the citizens of
the New Russia.

Peter's reforms set Russian architecture irrevocably in the western
mode. Not only did Russia now follow the major artistic movements
of the West – Baroque, Rococo, Classicism – but the very names of
the architects – Rastrelli, Rinaldi, Quarenghi, Vallin de la Mothe,
Velten, Cameron, Rossi – underline Russia's place in the international
artistic community. These names may suggest that there was little
'Russianness' left in Russian architecture, but this would be a mis-
apprehension, for these foreigners worked alongside Russians of no
lesser talent – Chevakinsky, Bazhenov, Kazakov, Starov, Voronikhin
– at a time when adherence to the ideal models of Classical antiquity
everywhere pushed national features into the background. But just as
in eleventh-century Kiev Byzantine conventions had been adapted to
local needs, in the eighteenth century Russia made the conventions
of Europe its own – be it in brightly painted exteriors, pediments in
wood or adaptations of the time-honoured five-dome church. But
then, as this chapter has sought to show, Russia already had several
centuries of experience to prepare her for the coming of the West.

CHAPTER III

European Images of Muscovy

SAMUEL H. BARON

West European diplomats, merchants, soldiers and technicians who either visited or resided in Muscovy in the sixteenth and seventeenth centuries doubtless registered many impressions, and some might even have ordered them into more or less coherent patterns. But obviously only if they committed their impressions and reflections to writings which were subsequently published could such individuals contribute to the western image of Russia. The question, What was the western image of Russia in these centuries?, must therefore be answered primarily with another question: What were then the most widely published works on the subject?

The two which assuredly take the palm are Baron Sigismund von Herberstein's *Rerum Moscoviticarum Commentarii* and Adam Olearius's *Neue Beschreibung der Muscowitischen und Persischen Reyse*. Herberstein's work, first published in 1549, went through some nineteen Latin, German, and Italian editions in the next 150 years, not counting extracts. Olearius's book first appeared in 1647, and the enlarged version printed in 1656 went through more than a score of German, French, English, Dutch, and Italian editions by the end of the century. The well-known English account, Giles Fletcher's *Of the Russe Commonwealth* (1591) is generally grouped with the other two as one of the three most important foreign reports on Muscovite Russia, even though it was published only three times in this period.

Herberstein, who went to Moscow on behalf of the Holy Roman Emperor in 1516–17 and 1525–6 (to mediate a conflict between Poland and Russia), has often been acclaimed as 'the discoverer of Russia'. He was so described because he wrote the first detailed, fairly comprehensive, and more or less systematic account of the Muscovite regime. And also because this regime, owing to a recent concatenation of events – the fall of the Byzantine Empire (1453), and overthrow of the Tartar yoke (1480), and the subsequent unification of many Russian principalities under the aegis of the Moscow princes – was in a sense a new realm, just emerging on to the European stage.

Unlike earlier writers on Russia, Herberstein was an eye-witness, and spent a full sixteen months in the country he wrote about; he was well educated, and had some facility with a Slavic language. Furthermore, as his mission was welcome to Moscow, he had unusual access to many highly-placed persons. These conditions help to explain the solidity of his work, which has long figured as the standard against which to judge other foreign accounts of Muscovy.

Although Herberstein produced a rather comprehensive account, only a sketch is needed to convey the salient features of his image of Russia. His single most important set of perceptions is this: 'In the sway that he holds over his people the ruler of Muscovy surpasses all the monarchs of the world.' He possesses 'unlimited control of the lives and property of his subjects' and 'all confess themselves to be his *Chlopos*, that is, serfs of the prince'. The word 'all' is not employed casually, for the prince 'uses his authority as much over ecclesiastics as laymen' and 'no one dares oppose him'. The awesome relationship of the people to their lord is expressed in their byword: 'The will of the prince is the will of God.' Even the greatest of the subjects obsequiously touch their heads to the ground before the

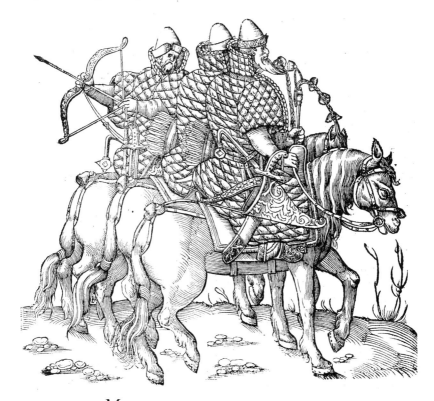

*M*ounted *Muscovite horsemen. From Herberstein's* Rerum Moscoviticarum *(1571 edition).*

ruler. Servile in relation to their master, the noblemen are in turn arrogant and domineering with respect to the common people, who are as serfs to them as well as to the prince.

Herberstein's implicit frame of reference, of course, was the western societies he knew, where, for all their diversity, nothing was to be found like the extraordinary power of the ruler, the subservience of the Church, the insignificance of the nobility, and the seemingly universal servitude in Muscovy. He arrestingly exposed to the western public a system unlike the contemporary monarchies of Europe, a system which would become known as Russian autocracy.

Herberstein offers no analysis of the origins of the system, but his account of the unscrupulous and brutal methods to which the Moscow princes resorted in their unification of the Russian lands hints that they appropriated the arbitrary, rapacious style of government of the former Tartar overlords, whom they had served while simultaneously aggrandizing themselves. The unification process carried out by Tsars Ivan III (1462–1505) and Vasily III (1505–33) is represented, not just as the conquest and expulsion of other princes from their domains, but as a sort of plague emanating from Moscow that strikes down and engulfs everything in its path. The case of Novgorod is most shockingly told. Ivan III attacked the city on false pretences and then 'despoiled the archbishop, the citizens, merchants and foreigners of all their goods'. Not content with that, he 'reduced all the inhabitants to abject servitude', deported all the leading citizens, and turned their lands over to the minions he sent to replace them. A further result of the catastrophe, the author observes, is that the people of Novgorod, who used to be courteous and honourable, 'now, doubtless from the Russian contagion introduced by people who emigrated from Moscow, are become most degraded'.

According to Herberstein, the common people of Muscovy are ruthlessly exploited, utterly defenceless, and morally degraded. The peasants must work six days a week on the land of their masters, and have but one day to till their own allotments. They must bear mistreatment uncomplainingly as they have no access to the prince and, in any case, 'all justice is venal'. The moral degradation of the people, as the nobleman Herberstein sees it, is manifested, among other ways, in their want of military valour. The Russians depend more on numbers than skill and discipline and, after attacking impetuously, they behave as if to say, If you do not flee, then we must. The Muscovites have no sense of honour; rulers routinely violate their solemn oaths.

In the conduct of business, the Muscovites are 'more cunning and deceitful than all others'. They engage in outrageous bargaining, and 'they swear with the very intention of deceiving'. Then Herberstein is repelled by the Russians' treatment of women. None is considered

Russorum Rex & Dominus sum, iure paterni
Sanguinis: imperij titulos à nemine, quauis
Mercatus prece, uel precio: nec legibus ullis
Subditus alterius, sed Christo credulus uni,
Emendicatos alijs aspernor honores.

'T sar Vasily III: image from Herberstein.

virtuous unless she lives shut up like a prisoner. Women are thought to be defiling, and so are seldom admitted into churches. Most surprisingly, married women regard beatings by their husbands as a measure of their love. Such evidence of a slavish disposition is not confined to women, for servants too complain if they do not receive a fair amount of beating. 'This people enjoys slavery more than freedom,' Herberstein declares in amazement, supporting the assertion with the observation that serfs who are manumitted immediately sell themselves again.

Is Herberstein's depiction of Muscovite ways truthful? It is certainly overdrawn in some respects. He misunderstood some of the phenomena he describes; and some other items he reported, for example that women take beatings as a sign of love, evoke scepticism. Needless to say, moreover, the diplomat's personal values coloured his portrayal, and his negative emphasis may in some measure have stemmed from talk heard at the Polish court before and after his visits to Moscow. Despite these failings, the work is to a large extent sound.

On the whole, it should be added, Herberstein uses restrained language in describing what he clearly finds distasteful in the people and mores of Muscovy. But on one occasion he gives vent to a memorable outburst that expresses his repugnance and perplexity:

> It is a matter of doubt whether the brutality of the people has made the prince a tyrant, or whether the people themselves have become brutal and cruel through the tyranny of the prince.

*T*he Winter Kingdom: Travel by sledge in Muscovy from
Herberstein.

No resolution of this conundrum occurs in Herberstein's *Commentarii*. The numerous editions of Herberstein's opus produced a strong influence on other writers on Russia. The Russian historian V.O. Klyuchevsky, author of a study of foreign accounts of the Muscovite state, observed, 'For most of the foreigners who wrote about Russia in the seventeenth, and even the last half of the sixteenth century, the works of earlier travellers to Muscovy served as the richest source. Much is borrowed, particularly from Herberstein and Olearius.' A more recent student, Andreas Kappeler, records that Herberstein's book was 'obligatory reading . . . for foreigners who seriously wished to understand the Muscovite state'. It was often used in the published works of others 'with or without citation', and so great was his authority that almost all subsequent writers followed him in giving the incorrect year (1528) as the birthdate of Ivan the Terrible.

Giles Fletcher travelled as Queen Elizabeth's envoy to Muscovy in 1588–9, to help to settle contentious issues which had arisen between the Russian court and the English Muscovy Company. An eventful sixty-year period intervened between Herberstein's visits and that of Fletcher. The Russia the latter describes therefore differs in important respects from the one Herberstein observed, but there are marked similarities as well. Fletcher's own summary of his findings, presented in the dedication of his treatise to Queen Elizabeth, may be rendered as follows: the Muscovite state is tyrannical; it is a regime without law or justice; the people are poor and oppressed – they are slaves rather than subjects; the Muscovites lack true knowledge of God. The last point has no precedent in the work of the Catholic Herberstein. Fletcher, a militant Protestant in an age of religious strife, relentlessly criticizes the Russian Church, whose beliefs and practices he repeatedly likens to those of the despised Papists. The other parts of the summary look quite familiar, impelling us to enquire whether this is a case of parallelism or of borrowing.

It is possible, of course, that Fletcher's depiction is similar to Herberstein's because both men were reporting on an external reality which each of them perceived in much the same way. However, a considerable amount of evidence can be adduced in support of the borrowing hypothesis. It is worth noting that Fletcher complained that he had been housed in Moscow 'as a prisoner, not an ambassador', a situation hardly conducive to wide-ranging personal observation or frank conversations with Russians. Accordingly, he was compelled to rely heavily on English residents in Moscow and published sources for information.

Fletcher was extraordinarily reticent on the subject of his sources, and nowhere does he mention Herberstein. Nevertheless, students of Fletcher's opus have gradually come to recognize that he knew Herberstein's book and borrowed from it at least a little. Richard

Pipes, one of the editors of a recent, facsimile edition of Fletcher, identified a total of twenty instances of probable borrowing from other authors, eight of them from Herberstein. He attributes no great significance to these borrowings though, indicating that Fletcher added them to an already well-turned manuscript based upon his observations and conversations with English residents in Russia that was much like the book published in 1591. (The 'well-turned' manuscript is now at Cambridge University.)

On a *limited* textological study however, nineteen additional cases of probable borrowing emerge (four more have been pinpointed by others), on a wide range of topics. Here are two examples, specially selected because they duplicate major features of Herberstein's image. While, according to Herberstein, the ruler 'holds unlimited control over the lives and property of all his subjects', Fletcher writes that the nobles now 'hold their authorities, lands, lives and all at the Emperor's pleasure, as the rest do'. Whereas Herberstein has all the Muscovites calling themselves '*Chlopos*, that is serfs of the prince', Fletcher refers to 'his *Kolophey*, that is, his very villeins or bondslaves'. Making positive identifications is occasionally difficult because Fletcher often rephrased considerably what he borrowed, as one author put it, 'to camouflage the origins of his knowledge'. It is noteworthy that Fletcher at least once repeats incorrect information found in Herberstein, namely that Vasily III (rather than Ivan III) was the first Muscovite ruler to take the title of emperor (tsar). Obviously, all this textological inquiry strengthens the brief for Herberstein's influence on Fletcher. It is still further strengthened by the discovery that all nineteen items were *already present* in the Cambridge manuscript, proof positive that Fletcher depended substantially on Herberstein as he composed this manuscript.

When did Fletcher first become acquainted with Herberstein's work, and had he read it before he journeyed to Muscovy? It is impossible to be certain, but it seems highly likely. By inclination and training, Fletcher was a scholar, and probably prepared himself for his mission more carefully than most envoys. No doubt he was briefed by royal and Muscovy Company officials; he probably studied documents relevant to his difficult mission, and he might also have gained access to the accounts by the company agents Richard Chancellor, Anthony Jenkinson, and Thomas Randolph, which characterized Russia as 'a rude and barbarous kingdom'. Whatever their merits, however, and they were not inconsiderable, these accounts could not have enjoyed the authority of Herberstein's work, which as early as 1571 had been published seven times in Latin and six times in other languages. If Herberstein was 'obligatory reading' for foreigners who seriously wished to understand the Muscovite state, Fletcher was just such a foreigner and it surely was mandatory for him. This very message was neatly put in a poem by an earlier

English traveller to Muscovy, George Turberville (written 1568–9, published 1587):

> . . . If thou list to know the Russies well
> To Sigismundus book repayre, who all the trueth can tell.

Fletcher might have read Turberville's poem, but he would not have needed its advice in order to be made aware of this far from obscure treatise. As T.S. Willan has written:

> Those Englishmen who not only went to Russia, but also wrote about that strange country, must have helped to create in the English mind some picture of the Russian political, economic, and social scene . . .; it was based on foundations laid by Sigismund von Herberstein.

This is not to insinuate that Fletcher slavishly copied Herberstein. There are many significant differences between the two works, and only some of them are to be explained by changed circumstances. Already noticed is the contrasting manner in which the two authors depicted Russian religion, and this holds for some other matters too. Besides, Fletcher has little or nothing to say on some topics Herberstein addressed; and, contrariwise, Fletcher treats in detail a number of matters which Herberstein either disregarded or dealt with very briefly, notably the organization and functioning of the state apparatus. Fletcher emphasizes much more than his predecessor popular shortcomings such as the prevalence of ignorance and superstition and the penchant for unbridled drinking ('to drink drunk is an ordinary matter with them every day in the week'). Fletcher's work is distinctly more systematic than Herberstein's. Finally, he is decidedly more concerned than his predecessor to probe for the causes and interrelations of the phenomena he observes, so that he succeeds better in articulating disparate elements into a meaningful whole. *Of the Russe Commonwealth* is full of information and reflections which have won it a well-deserved reputation as an extremely valuable source.

On the other hand, if Fletcher almost certainly read Herberstein before he voyaged to Moscow; if, in composing the Cambridge manuscript, he consulted Herberstein again, and plainly borrowed much material from him; and if, after completing the Cambridge manuscript, he returned to Herberstein to draw yet again on this mine of information for the final draft of his work, one has every reason to state that Herberstein was a major source for Fletcher. Moreover, if at these key stages in the conception and composition of his work, Fletcher was intimately involved with Herberstein, and if his image of Russia, although much elaborated and better systemized, is strikingly similar to Herberstein's, the conclusion cannot be avoided that Fletcher's image of Russia owed a great deal to Herberstein. Of course Fletcher was anxious to conceal the

To the Queenes moſt ex-
cellent *Maieſtie*.

Oſt gracious
Soueraigne,
beeyng em-
ployed in
your Maie-
ſties ſeruice
to the Em-
perour of *Ruſſia*, I obſerued the
State, and manners of that Coun-
trey . And hauing reduced the
ſame into ſome order , by the
way as I returned, I haue preſu-
med to offer it in this ſmal Booke
to your moſt excellent Maieſtie.
My meaning was to note thinges
for mine owne experience, of
more importaunce then delight,
and rather true then ſtrange . In
their maner of gouernment, your
Highneſſe may ſee both : A true
and ſtrange face of a *Tyrannical ſtate,*
(moſt vnlike to your own) with
out true knowledge of G O D,
without written Lawe, without
common iuſtice : ſaue that which
proceedeth from their *Speaking
Lawe*, to wit, the Magiſtrate who
hath moſt neede of a Lawe, to re-
ſtraine his owne iniuſtice . The
practiſe hereof as it is heauy , and
grieuous to the poore oppreſſed
people , that liue within thoſe
Countreyes : ſo it may giue iuſt
cauſe to my ſelfe , and other your
Maieſties faithfull ſubiects , to ac-
knowledge our happines on this
behalfe , and to giue God thankes
for your Maieſties moſt Prince-
like, and gracious gouernment : as
alſo to your Highneſſe more ioy,
and contentment in your royall
eſtate, in that you are a Prince of
ſubiectes, not of ſlaues, that are
kept within ductie by loue, not
by feare. The Almightie ſtil bleſſe
your Highnes with a moſt long,
and happy reigne in this life,
and with Chriſt Ieſus in
the life to come.

*Your Maieſties moſt honble
ſubiect, and ſeruant*

*D*edication to Elizabeth I by Giles Fletcher from his own Of the
Russe Commonwealth *(1591), drawing a tactful contrast between
the 'constitutional' Gloriana and the 'tyrannical' Ivan the Terrible.*

connection, and to impress upon his readers the complete originality of his work. So well did he accomplish this feat that four centuries passed before his stratagem was brought to light.

One last point. Pipes observes that 'One of the principal premises and conclusions of Fletcher's account is that tyranny breeds barbarism.' With this proposition there can be no quarrel, but how can we not recognize Fletcher's formulation for what it is? The conundrum posed by Herberstein had quite surely caught his attention and, whether consciously or unconsciously, one of the chief aims of his book was to solve the enigma that had stumped Herberstein.

Adam Olearius sojourned in Muscovy three times in the 1630s as a member of embassies dispatched by the Duke of Holstein to negotiate treaties expected to win control of the lucrative Persian silk trade for Holstein. Like Fletcher's, Olearius's book may be thought of as (among other things) an updating and amplification of Herberstein. Olearius stands at the opposite pole from Fletcher, however, in freely (if not fully) acknowledging his indebtedness to other sources. He appended a lengthy bibliography to his work, and his text abounds in references to volumes he had drawn upon. Far and away the most prominent of these is Herberstein, whom he refers to twenty-one times.

Olearius was obviously much influenced by Herberstein, but did he derive his image of Russia from his predecessor? As I wrote in my introduction to the 1967 edition of Olearius, the salient features of Olearius's portrait are 'political tyranny, moral debasement, and indifference or hostility to intellectual pursuits'. As befits an intellectual, Olearius emphasized and elaborated the last of the three much more than Herberstein, but the other points are key items in Herberstein's characterization of Muscovite society. Olearius dwells much more on qualities of the people which he finds repellent and, much less inhibited than Herberstein, he flatly asserts, 'When you observe the spirit, the mores, and the way of life of the Russians, you are bound to number them among the barbarians.' The words and phrases he employs in respect to the Russians' purported want of valour, unscrupulousness in trade, treatment of women and their slavish disposition are strikingly similar to Herberstein's. Perhaps not just coincidentally, most of this material occurs in passages where no source is cited.

The same may be said of Olearius's representation of the Muscovite political order. The essential features, though more amplified than in Herberstein, are plainly those that the latter first etched. The tsar is the undisputed master of the country and its inhabitants; the people, whether of high or low degree, are his slaves and serfs; they recognize his will as the will of God, and their possessions as his property. We may be certain that the *Commentarii* lay before Olearius as he composed the sections of his book on the tsar and his powers.

But while Olearius clearly held Herberstein in great esteem, he was not uncritical. He corrected him on various matters, notably when he labels incredible Herberstein's allegation that Russian women take beatings by their husbands as a token of love. Similarly, he attempted to distance himself from Herberstein with respect to the political order:

> Although they possess the same power, the most recent grand princes have not emulated the former tyrants, who violently assaulted their subjects' property. Yet some of our contemporaries hold to the contrary view, perhaps basing themselves on old writers such as Herberstein . . . who depicted the Russians' miserable condition under the tyrants' sceptre. In general, a great deal is written about the Russians which no longer applies, undoubtedly because of general changes in time, regime, and people.

Of course, Olearius deserves credit for his effort to be sensitive to changed circumstances. But the few scattered remarks of a positive kind that he makes about Tsars Mikhail and Alexis are far outweighed by his emphasis on the atrocities committed by former rulers, the extravagant power the present ruler still possesses (he calls the polity a 'dominating and despotic monarchy'), and the servility of the people. Whatever his intentions, therefore, Olearius's work (undoubtedly the most widely-read treatise on Russia in the seventeenth century) reinforced and perpetuated Herberstein's image of Russia.

To sum up, Herberstein's *Rerum Moscoviticarum Commentarii*, the first great foreign work on Muscovite Russia, drew a distinctive socio-political order which stood in sharp contrast to west European societies on critical counts. Because the author was well qualified and his account unprecedentedly detailed, comprehensive and persuasive, it was immediately recognized as a classic. Understandably, it exercised a powerful influence on subsequent writers on Muscovy – among them Fletcher and Olearius.

It is necessary to distinguish between two relevant issues: the borrowing of discrete pieces of information and the adoption, whether consciously or otherwise, of a more or less articulated image. It is of course easier to demonstrate borrowing of the first than the second kind. The images projected by all three writers, though not identical, indisputably have a great deal in common (though by itself this proves nothing). But now that we know as well that Fletcher and Olearius were intimately familiar with Herberstein's opus and couched their descriptions of major features of Muscovy in terms much like his, the issue of appropriation cannot be avoided.

It may be impossible to prove beyond a shadow of a doubt that Fletcher and Olearius derived their image of Russia from Herberstein, but it is at least highly probable that their images were significantly shaped by the imperial diplomat's pioneering work. The two later

An Easter procession in Red Square. From Olearius's Voyages
(1657 edition).

writers ratified and thus helped to ensure the continued prevalence in Europe of that mode of envisaging Russia which Herberstein had inaugurated.

In fact Herberstein's influence, whether direct or indirect, extended well beyond 1700. His image of Russia had made so indelible an impression that it continued well beyond that point to shape the way west Europeans thought about the great realm in the East. Moreover, in the twentieth century, more particularly since the end of the Second World War, Herberstein's work has enjoyed a striking revival. At least six editions in five languages appeared between 1951 and 1967. No doubt this surge of interest is to be explained, at least in part, by the Cold War, which in our time has emphasized once again the contrasts between Russia and the West.

CHAPTER IV

Tsar Alexis goes to War

PHILIP LONGWORTH

In May, 1654, the second Romanov Tsar, Alexis Mikhailovich, rode out from Moscow to make war against the state of Poland-Lithuania. It was a scene of medieval brilliance. The young Tsar – he was only twenty-five – was preceded by a forest of banners, including his personal standard sewn with gold with its double-headed eagle and the motto, 'Fear God and Obey the Tsar'. He and his retainers were dressed magnificently – even the hoofs of his horse were set with pearls – and he was followed by a huge and glittering retinue. The towering figure of Nikon, the Patriarch of Moscow, sprinkled holy water over them and on the serried ranks of warriors as they passed. Thus began a series of campaigns that was to mark Russia's emergence as a major European power. It was also to change Alexis' own perceptions of the world, his ambitions, his tastes – and inaugurate, albeit indirectly, a decisive stage in the westernization of Russia.

Alexis went to war as an old-fashioned crusader. Given the nature of his upbringing, this is hardly surprising. His education had been heavily oriented towards religion; the church calendar dictated his annual round of fasting, feasting and pilgrimages – besides which, as he understood very well, a tsar's open profession of his piety, humility and charity was a powerful confirmation of his legitimacy in the eyes of his people. More recently, Alexis had also been influenced by Orthodox churchmen from the Ukraine and the Ottoman Empire. They had been urging him to regard himself as 'a new Moses' who would 'liberate pious and Orthodox Christians from the unclean hands' of Catholic or Muslim rulers. Certainly this was the role he now assumed in offering his protection to the Orthodox Ukrainians in their fight against Catholic Poland and in setting out to recapture the Russian city of Smolensk (a task at once holy and patriotic) which the Poles had occupied since 1611.

The memorandum which Alexis had drafted over a year before, when the decision to go to war had been taken, clearly reflected his overriding religious faith. 'On military affairs,' it began, 'How to protect the true, Orthodox Christian faith . . . and the holy ecumenical Church, and all Orthodox Christians.' More recently, he had prepared for campaign with a round of pilgrimages to holy shrines, by ordering the release of treasured icons to inspire his soldiers in

*T*sar Alexis, a portrait, 1657, by S. Loputsky.

battle, and by bombarding his generals with homilies warning them
that victory would only come as a reward for the army's chastity
and piety; that defeat would be the consequence of sin. 'When battle
begins,' he told Prince Trubetskoi, 'you and your men are to go
forth on God's business singing . . . Keep the Jesus prayer in mind
. . . Go into battle joyfully, without any doubting, and your singing
will be such that despite yourselves . . . you will not be defeated
. . . and will seem terrible to all the enemy.' Every soldier was to
fast and take communion in preparation for the fighting – to ensure
that 'the Angel of the Lord will take up arms' on their behalf.

Faith in the cause has always been a powerful moral factor in war, of course, but Alexis seems to have ranked it above all else as a means of gaining victory – just as he believed that all the disasters that had afflicted his country in the troubled half-century preceding were somehow due to his subjects' impiety and to wrong religion, to Russians praying in an incorrect way. It was on this account that he had recently ordered the imposition of wide-ranging liturgical reforms designed to bring Russian Church practices and texts into line with their Greek originals – to the great consternation of traditionalists. No wonder, then, that so many of Alexis' courtiers referred to him disparagingly behind his back, calling him 'the young monk'.

The slight was soon to vanish from their lips, however, for he was to emerge from this war a changed man. The three years of campaigning he was now embarking on were to be his university. They were to immerse him in a whole range of practical and urgent problems; they were to take him to foreign lands and expose him to their cultures; and, not least, they were to distance him from the Kremlin – liberate him from the trammels of court life, from the influence of prelates, and, much though he loved his wife and sisters, from the claustrophobic embrace of family life. Indeed, on 6 July, just eight days after he arrived outside Smolensk, he dictated a message to his family apologizing for not writing a letter in his own hand since 'I have no time and am very busy'.

He was indeed. Besides keeping in touch with affairs in Moscow, where a commission of boyars was running day-to-day business, and corresponding with his regent, the Patriarch Nikon – not least about the dispatch to the front of supplies, horses and men from church estates – he was immersed in the task of trying to co-ordinate the operations of three Russian armies and the Ukrainian Cossack forces which were operating over a vast area. And he was also following the siege of Smolensk itself with close attention. This much is evident from the thirty-nine notebooks on military matters which he filled.

Smolensk was defended by high walls, a mile and a half in circumference. It had thirty-eight towers, not all of them in good repair, and a motley garrison of some 3,500 men. The Tsar's 30,000 troops heavily outnumbered them. Nevertheless, the task of capturing this stronghold was to prove by no means easy. For several weeks Alexis was in constant consultation about the matter with his generals – among them the eighty-year-old veteran of many a siege, General Alexander Leslie, an artillery and engineering specialist. Leslie had begun the preparations for the siege before the Tsar's arrival, choosing positions for the guns as they were trundled up, setting the lines along which saps and trenches were to be dug and supervising the construction of mobile fortifications. Since Alexis' arrival the bombardment of Smolensk had grown heavier by the day. Some of its bastions were demolished, but still the garrison held firm. Soon news arrived of the continuing advances made by the other Russian forces; then that they had captured the city of Polotsk – but still Smolensk resisted, and it was the middle of August before everything was ready for a general storm.

The storming operation failed. The jubilant defenders claimed to have killed 7,000 Russians and wounded 15,000 more. No doubt they exaggerated – but the casualties were serious enough. A week was to pass before Alexis summoned up sufficient courage to inform his family about it. 'We lost three hundred men killed and a thousand wounded,' he wrote – then, anxious not to depress his sisters and his wife too much, he added a postscript: 'Do not grieve about the storm. Our men fought stoutly and famously, and beat them.' But for all his faith that death in so holy a cause would open up the doors of Heaven to the victims, the sight of the carnage had obviously troubled him. From that time on he was to take a more tolerant view of cowards. 'Courage,' he was to remark, 'is not given to every man alike.'

Eventually Smolensk did fall, though through attrition rather than assault. Early in September its commander asked for terms; five days later the city gates were opened. Alexis entered with considerable pomp and wearing his regalia to accept the allegiance of the inhabitants. The campaign of 1654 had achieved all he had expected. His forces had overrun a large part of Belorussia, including the city of Vitebsk, and had penetrated Lithuania. Greater prizes seemed likely to fall into his hands in the next campaigning season. On the other hand, disturbing news was reaching him of a severe outbreak of the plague in Moscow. Alexis' family and the Patriarch had been evacuated in time, but thousands of all classes had already died; many had fled in panic and spread the plague elsewhere before quarantine barriers

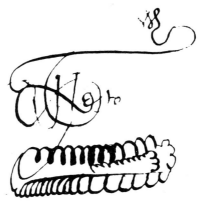

Cover of Alexis' notebook On Military Affairs *(1653), showing the Tsar's personal monogram with a doodling drawn in his own hand.*

could be set up; and the survivors were in an angry mood. Traditionalists were blaming the plague on the church reforms; Nikon, the Patriarch, was being reviled for deserting Moscow. It looked for a time as if Alexis might have as serious a public order crisis on his hands as he had had to cope with in 1648 when there had been a general rising in Moscow against his government.

Yet for all the disruption and depopulation caused by the plague, Alexis determined to resume military operations as soon as the weather permitted. He was not a man to abandon his ambitions lightly. Besides, plundering the Poles might compensate for Russia's losses, and he felt himself to be on a winning streak. This fact is evident from his reaction to a meeting at Viazma that autumn with an envoy from Charles X of Sweden, who at that time controlled a large part of the southern Baltic shoreline, including Riga, gateway to the West – regions adjacent to the Russians' lines of advance.

'I have not seen such a stupid envoy in ten years,' Alexis wrote to his friend and confidant Artamon Matveev, who commanded a regiment of his Praetorian Guard, the strel'tsy. 'This fool,' he continued,

> was sent to find out what we are prepared to do for love of the King. But the Swedes are very frightened of us . . . not so much on account of Smolensk as on account of Vitebsk and Polotsk, because of our occupying the route along the Dvina to Riga . . . The King writes that . . . he is sending his ambassador to us (and a high-ranking counsellor at that) . . . as if for love of me . . . But we know how much his so-called love prompted him. It was fear rather.

The King had asked him 'not to invade Courland for the sake of [our] friendship for his majesty, because [the Duke of] Courland is a friend [of his] . . . But . . . [we] rejected this on the grounds that he [Courland] is a subject of the Polish King.' For once God and the saints found no mention. This was a new Alexis, a realist possessed of an unaccustomed confidence, not to say arrogance, bred of his success in war.

Having spent only a few weeks with his family at Viazma on 11 March 1655, he set off for the front again, despite terrible weather conditions. ('The road is so bad,' he wrote, 'I have never seen a worse one in my life.') It took him nineteen days to reach Smolensk, his operational base. There he received another ambassador, this time from Venice – the first ever sent by the Republic to a tsar of Muscovy. Recognition was sweet; and the Venetian brocade and the fine Venetian glass which were among the gifts the ambassador brought him were also much appreciated. But Alexis would not be deflected by his offer of an alliance against the Turks. For the moment at least his sights were set firmly towards the West, towards Wilno (now Vilnius), the ancient capital of Lithuania. He reached it in July in time to see its capture on the 29th. Next day he made a triumphant entrance sitting in a finc French, brown-upholstered carriage driven by a coachman in brown and yellow livery and flanked by a bodyguard dressed in brown and red. A red carpet had been laid down for him; a gun salute boomed out.

The successes continued. His troops took Kovno (now Kaunas), then Grodno. Virtually all of Lithuania, half the Polish Kingdom, was now in his hands. But by then the Swedes had entered the war. They had moved into Poland's Baltic provinces in July, and were pressing on towards Warsaw and Cracow. The Polish King took refuge in Silesia; Poland-Lithuania was at the point of collapse.

Alexis stayed all summer at Wilno pondering these developments, and the outcome of his deliberations was a surprising reversal of policy: an alliance with Catholic Poland against the Swedes. By this, Alexis hoped to force his way through Livonia to gain an outlet to the Baltic and so enrich his country by gaining direct trading contact with the West; he also hoped to gain the elective crown of Poland when the present King should die or abdicate – an ambition, which, as he could not have failed to recognize, must imply some concessions from him, the standard-bearer of the true orthodoxy, to the heretical Catholics.

Perhaps the atmosphere of Wilno influenced him as much as strategic considerations. Wilno was a considerable centre of culture which seemed excitingly strange and western to Muscovite eyes – it still does today. Certainly the material culture of the city, its architecture and artefacts, intrigued the Tsar. He could not resist the marble columns and pavements of Prince Radziwill's beautiful palace there. He had them sent off to Moscow, along with the gilding from its seven cupolas. Alexis, the conqueror, had himself been taken captive by the lures of an alien civilization.

The plague having abated, Alexis returned to Moscow in September, though he set out yet again in Ascension week 1656 – this time with the aim of advancing up the River Dvina towards Riga and the Baltic. His route on this occasion lay through Polotsk, another ancient centre of culture and learning, and it was there that he allowed himself to be declared King-elect of Poland. From Polotsk he crossed into Livonia, reaching the Swedish citadel of Dünabork on 24 July. A week later he was outside Riga.

Riga was the great prize – a thriving Hanseatic port, a major centre for international trade, a springboard to western Europe. It was, however, well defended, and by now the Russians' lines of communications were severely stretched. Day by day, week by week, the city was subjected to heavy cannon and mortar fire. But this time Alexis was out of luck. The Swedes conducted a successful sally; most of the boats the Russians brought up the river were destroyed, and the garrison could not be cut off from reinforcements. The siege dragged into its third month, the Russians, increasingly short of supplies and suffering heavy losses and privations; a song about their travails at the siege was still being sung in Russia a century later. Early in October with the cold already biting sharply, the siege had to be abandoned. A crestfallen Alexis made his way back to Polotsk.

Alexis was never again to go on campaign. The wars, however, were to continue for more than a decade, bringing ever more severe misfortunes. Wilno was to be lost in 1660; the Ukraine fell into anarchy; Alexis was never to gain the crown of Poland and his subsequent attempt to procure it for his son Feodor was also to fail. True, Smolensk, Belorussia, the eastern Ukraine and Kiev were to remain in Russian hands – a substantial achievement. But despite these successes and the plunder of the first three years, the costs of war were heavy. Spending on weapons, munitions and the pay of foreign mercenaries was huge; so was the disruption to the

*M*ap of Poland, circa 1654.

Russian economy. The government had been forced to start issuing copper coins in place of silver ones early in the war, and the money supply increased sharply thereafter, promoting galloping inflation. Discontent was to grow in proportion, culminating in defections, riots, and the damaging insurrection of 1670–1. The monarchy was to survive these troubles, though the Church was to suffer. It bore a large part of the costs of war, being obliged to pay forced loans and supply vast numbers of men and animals, huge quantities of food and other supplies. And though Alexis was never to forsake the Orthodox faith (legitimizing, as it did, his own authority as tsar) or abandon the liturgical reforms, he soon broke with his old friend Nikon. The Church ceased to be an independent power in the land.

The war also changed Alexis himself. He had lost his innocence, and gained new insights, on those three campaigns. Wilno and Polotsk had opened his eyes to the possibility of moulding a new, imperial environment for himself. As one of his personal physicians, the Englishman Samuel Collins, was to write, since the Tsar had 'seen the manner of the Princes' houses' in other countries 'and guessed at the modes of their kings, his thoughts are more advanced and he begins to furnish his rooms with tapestry, and contrive houses of pleasure abroad'.

Certainly, within a matter of months, dozens, perhaps hundreds, of foreign craftsmen and artists were brought to Muscovy – furniture-makers, leather-embossers, woodcarvers, painters; and in 1658 the design of his new apartments was entrusted to another foreigner, the engineer Gustav Dekenpin. Its dininghall was to be decorated with carving, gilded, and have murals painted 'in the new foreign style'. Thereafter, the style of the baroque became ever more evident – though, anxious not to arouse the hostility of the tradition-bound masses unnecessarily, Alexis was careful to keep the exteriors of his new buildings free of substantial innovations. He also had his portrait painted in the realistic western style and wore clothes cut in the Polish manner. He even had his son Feodor taught Polish. But the extent of his new readiness to accept western technology and consider western ideas is reflected in the commissions he gave to his English buying agent in western Europe, John Hebdon, between 1657 and 1659.

He ordered silver caskets from him, dishes, plates, knives, forks and fingerbowls; trees for his gardens, three fine carriages (of which only two were supplied), Spanish-style uniforms in which to dress his palace guard, armchairs, even a glass summer-house. Nor was his enthusiasm restricted to western luxuries. In February 1659, he ordered the engagement abroad of 'a first-class doctor who can cure with herbs . . . a first-class alchemist . . . who understands the properties of herbs and knows how to dispense; a reliable herbal book . . .; experts in silver, copper and iron ores; . . . a German spring-maker; a book for the Artillery Department, a book on firing upwards' (perhaps about trajectories) 'monthly news from all states; good birds' (including singing parrots and canaries) 'master glass-makers who can manufacture transparent glass' and who knew where the raw materials for such glass were to be found.

Military wants ranked high in view of the importance now attached to the building up of a fully modernized army. He ordered a 'military book' which would explain the theory of warfare: how to make fire-plans, how to storm, besiege and defend towns, how best to organize a baggage train. He wanted to enlist 'the very best colonels and scholars of military formation . . . and able master gunners who can direct fire both from heights and on the flat, at long range and accurately'. He called for an 'eye-glass, such as when approaching a town one can see everything in it', and for 'little observation tubes . . . through which to look out from a trench and which one can squeeze in one's hand so that it should not be visible' (a polemoscopium, or trench periscope).

By the time he died, at the early age of forty-seven, he had accumulated a small library of military works – plans of how to draw up regiments in the 'German style', drawings of bombs, grenades and guns; and he had engaged thousands of foreign mercenaries – Germans, Austrians, Danes and Frenchmen, and many Englishmen, Irishmen and Scots as well (including Thomas Dalyell and Patrick Gordon). But beyond that, as an eighteenth-century military historian rightly remarked, Alexis founded the first Russian permanent standing army to be organized and trained 'according to the rules of military science'. He was also the first Russian to try to build a modern navy and to found a merchant fleet.

All this and more suggests that Alexis' going to war in 1654 may have marked a major stage in the westernization of Russia. Certainly his experiences on campaign sharpened his curiosity about the West, and led him to acquire more western books on non-military subjects than any of his predecessors – books on ancient history, hydraulics, biology and cosmography. How much he learned from them it is impossible to say for he knew no foreign language, but he became very anxious in later life to project an image of himself abroad as a civilized monarch, inclined – in the words of his ambassador to France and Spain – 'to many learned and philosophical sciences'.

The claim, inspired as it was by dynastic ambitions and the desire to gain acceptance among his European peers, was no doubt inflated. Yet he had been fired with a genuine enthusiasm for knowledge. This led him not only to indulge in the intellectual vogue current in the Europe of that time to seek out oddities of all kinds, but also to improve agriculture (especially on his own estates), to found new industries (including two glass factories), to sponsor western arts (including ultimately the theatre and the ballet) and to encourage the propagation of science – he founded a school of medicine in

The Patriarch Nikon, a painting circa 1660.

the Kremlin at which young Russians were trained to western professional standards. His interests, however, were overwhelmingly
practical rather than abstract – directed, whether directly or indirectly, towards improving his country's economic health and military
strength. He would not tolerate freethinking or dissent among his
people; nor did he show interest in western political ideas, though
Hobbes, if not Milton, might have appealed to him. On the other

hand, he had come to set his face very firmly against those of his subjects – and they were many – who rejected any manifestation of 'foreign cunning', as they termed any unwelcome intrusion from 'the godless West'.

This is not to claim of course that Alexis initiated the westernization process. Ivan IV had forged strong links with England and Denmark, and engaged a Florentine architect to work on the Kremlin. The unfortunate Boris Godunov had been a westernizer, though he had long since been discredited. Foreigners had been tempted into the Russian service long before Alexis came to rule – though never on such a scale. Their influence on Russia was to be proportionate to their numbers, even though it took time to seep through and their cultural impact on the masses was to be slight. The seed of Russia's westernization may have already germinated, then, but it was a very sickly plant before Alexis' time. When he died in 1676, he had steered at least the élite of his people away from Byzantine exclusiveness and stagnation, and done more than any of his predecessors to turn the face of Russia westwards (certainly as much as his people could tolerate or absorb). From his time onwards, the process of modernization had become irreversible, as had Russia's emergence as a world power.

It is strange, then, that historians should have masked this achievement. They have either idealized Alexis as the representative figure of the old Russian culture, or played down his significance in order to promote the reputation of his youngest son, Peter the Great. Yet it was Alexis who set the precedents for almost all Peter's reforms. Indeed it is impossible to imagine Peter succeeding to the extent that he did had it not been for his father's work. It is time these facts were recognized. And when they are, it seems probable that Alexis' going to war in 1654 will emerge as one of the significant turning-points in the history of eastern Europe.

CHAPTER V

Muscovy looks West

MARC RAEFF

The Russian epic hero, Ilia Muromets, sat paralysed for thirty years, unable to get up from his seat or use his hands. One day, when his parents had gone to the fields and left him sitting in front of his house, three pilgrims came up and asked him for a drink of water and food. When he told them that he could not get up and fetch it, they ordered him to stand up and to bring the water – and lo, behold, he did get up and draw water from the well. The pilgrims told him to drink the water and so he did, they then asked him how he felt. 'If there were a ring attached to the world,' he said, 'I would overturn the whole world.' The pilgrims ordered him to drink some more and this time Ilia Muromets felt his strength halved; the pilgrims went away and the young hero set forth from his house to do valiant battle for Prince Vladimir, the Beautiful Sun, of Kiev.

One is reminded of this story in connection with the stunning effect produced in Europe by the emergence of Russia as a leading military power following Peter I's victory over Charles XII at Poltava in 1709. Let us then take the epic as a literary conceit to guide us in understanding the dramatic appearance of a new political and military giant on the European stage.

Up to about the middle of the seventeenth century, with some rare and insignificant exceptions, 'medieval' Russia, or Muscovy, had existed in relative isolation from Central and Western Europe; even with its immediate neighbours, Poland and Sweden, there had hardly been much cultural and economic exchange. After the so-called Time of Troubles (1605–13), while licking the wounds inflicted by war, social anarchy, and economic collapse, Moscow had turned more xenophobic and isolationist. While Muscovy recovered from the worst effects of the Time of Troubles, it fell into permanent crisis – religious, dynastic, socio-economic, cultural – in the course of the second half of the seventeenth century. Muscovy was becoming progressively paralysed, unable to resolve the conflicts that were racking its body social and politic; at any rate unable to cope with the help of those traditional institutional and 'ideological' means which, in the fifteenth and sixteenth centuries, had enabled Moscow to assert its primacy over all Russian lands, build a powerful military and political organization, and develop a sophisticated religious culture.

Thus, by the last decade of the seventeenth century, Muscovy seemed to be a giant (for let us not forget that it was the largest compact territorial state in Europe) condemned to passivity and ossification. And there was no relief in sight, for traditionalist Muscovite society was not able to provide any viable alternatives; and its continuing existence appeared to be due less to its own vital energy than to its neighbours' weakness and disinterest.

In fact, however, there was a silent stirring, the water in the well was being refreshed by new underground streams, and soon it would become a miraculous draught to vivify the paralysed body of the Muscovite polity. Adumbrated first by Ivan IV (1533–84) and Boris Godunov (1598–1605), and pursued more consistently since the reign of Tsar Alexis (1645–76), the father of Peter I, Moscow's policy had been turning away from its traditional fixation on the East (and South-East), where it aimed at taking the place of the Mongol 'empire of the steppes'. Muscovy was now definitely seeing its main foreign policy tasks in the West (and South-West). This was partly due to the internal weakening of Poland and Moscow's growing involvement in the diplomatic and military affairs of East Central Europe. But in some measure it was also the result of the economic aggressiveness of Dutch and English merchants. Indeed, by way of Archangel, these enterprising traders were bringing western luxury and technical goods for the Kremlin's élite; in return they obtained Russian raw materials and eastern merchandise.

Russia's greater involvement in European wars required borrowing new techniques and tactics. The traditional mounted noble 'militia' that had been the backbone of the Tsar's military establishment had to give way to the so-called 'newly formed regiments' – units of professional soldiers, officered mainly by foreigners, and equipped with modern weapons. In short, a sizeable group of foreigners, settled for economic or military purposes, had become a fixed and significant

The foreign quarter in Moscow. A seventeenth-century engraving.

element of Muscovy. Although the foreigners had to reside in a separate section (the foreign suburb – *nemetskaia sloboda*) of the capital, they took an active part in the daily life of Moscow. Increasingly, members of the Tsar's immediate entourage manifested curiosity for things west European, but they also endeavoured to acquire the cultural perquisites of a 'European' way of life. However, they did so cautiously and selectively, without abandoning their traditional and religious outlook and customs.

In paying greater attention to the West, the Muscovite state had also become more interested in what was happening in the European states – and vice versa, of course, central and west European diplomats and rulers were becoming more curious about Muscovy. The Tsar's realm was seen not only as a possible ally in military and diplomatic schemes, but also as a land where western experiences and training might find useful and remunerative application. Many a German – or Dutch or Scottish – artisan, university graduate, or technician proved willing to settle (permanently or temporarily) in Moscow after failing to find a steady career in Europe. Many military men found employment in Moscow when circumstances forced them to leave their homeland (men like Patrick Gordon from Scotland or Franz Lefort from Geneva).

Moscow's curiosity for the happenings in the West led to the sending of embassies to the major European states. The ambassadors' reports quite clearly show not only their authors' bewilderment, but also their earnest efforts to inform themselves and to understand the diverse institutional, economic, social and cultural arrangements they observed on their mission. In addition to these embassies, the authorities in the Kremlin collected and 'abstracted' European gazettes, and summaries of the information thus gathered was circularized in print, in the so-called *Kuranty*.

West European intellectual achievements penetrated into Muscovy in a somewhat unexpected way. Political and ecclesiastical developments in the late sixteenth century had made possible the infiltration of the Catholic Counter-Reformation into lands that had originally been exclusively Orthodox. To the Orthodox Church in the Ukraine, with its historical, spiritual, and intellectual centre at Kiev, it became obvious that to stem Catholic proselytism it was necessary to forge intellectual tools capable of countering Catholic arguments and educational efforts. This need led to a renaissance of theological and liturgical literature written by clergy from Kiev or the Ukraine in general.

One of the consequences of this effort was the ritual reforms of Patriarch Nikon in the Russian Church and the resulting split with the Old Believers that destroyed the traditional religious-political consensus of the Muscovite polity; it was a significant factor of the paralysis of Moscow mentioned earlier.

СТѢЙШІЙ КУРЪ ѲИЛАРЕТЪ НИКИТІЧЬ ПАТРІАРХЪ МОСКОВСКІЙ И ВСЕѦ РОССІИ.

The Patriarch Filaret Romanov, as father of Tsar Mikhail (1613–45) played a leading role in politics after the Time of Troubles.

Of particular significance from our perspective here was the Ukrainian and Belorussian Orthodox clergy's realization that they had to renew their homiletic and apologetic armoury with the implements fashioned in the West and which were so effectively used by their Catholic – primarily Jesuit – opponents. And so it was that the first East Slavic institution of 'higher ecclesiastic learning' was founded by Peter Mohyla, Metropolitan of Kiev, in 1632. This Academy became the centre for the intensive and modern training of the clerical élite, and it also stimulated the development of a network of schools in the Ukraine that were open to the laity as well. Furthermore, far from contenting itself with providing instruction in Kiev, the Academy arranged for more advanced study of its graduates at university centres in Western and Central Europe.

In this way intellectual movements prevailing in Europe were assimilated by the best of the Ukranian clergy in the course of the seventeenth century. Little wonder that these clergymen were highly regarded in the Eastern Slavic Orthodox world, in particular in Moscow.

The incorporation of the Ukraine into the Muscovite state in the mid-seventeenth century only intensified these ecclesiastical and intellectual contacts. By the late seventeenth century Kiev-trained clergy had established the Slavonic-Greek-Latin Academy in Moscow and such individuals as Epifanii Slavinetskii and Simeon Polotskii had become the dominant intellectual force in Moscow, participating in the education of the Tsar's children and of the younger generation of the Kremlin élite. We know now that even the clerks of the central government institutions of Moscow (*prikazy*), particularly the Office of Ambassadors (*posol'skii prikaz* – the 'foreign office') acquired some basic European intellectual-philosophical tools, not to speak of languages such as Latin, and were actively involved in the creation of a new secular and poetic literature that circulated in manuscript form among the élite.

Finally, such outstanding and influential individuals as the head of the Office of Ambassadors, A.L. Ordyn-Nashchokin, the Tsar's tutor Artamon Matveev, and others had been exposed, and to a large part had assimilated these western intellectual currents by the end of Tsar Alexis' reign. By the late seventeenth century there was a significant minority of individuals in the capital – both native and foreign – who were interested in and capable of acquiring European models for intellectual as well as political reasons. What new source could now be tapped? It turned out to be the new political culture that had been taking shape in the West in the course of the seventeenth century, especially since the end of the Thirty Years War. It may be summarily defined as the administrative practices of the 'Well ordered police state' (*état policé, ordentlicher Policeystaat*); a reorientation of the purpose and character of government and specifically of administrative action. From having been conceived in the past in negative terms – defence against the outside enemy and maintenance of law for domestic security – government now acquired the positive function of organizing and disciplining society (or select sectors of it) for the purpose of maximizing productivity, so as to increase the power and prosperity of both state (monarch) and people.

63

To this end the numbers of administrative officers were increased and trained so as to transmute knowledge into action to shape social conduct and make it more productive. It provided a new ideal type or guide of action for the governments of Europe and resulted in the rise of modern, functionally organized administrations, the growth of codification, and the state's expanding involvement in economic, social and cultural pursuits. The socio-economic as well as intellectual and cultural progress of the eighteenth century (often subsumed under the categories of the Enlightenment and the agrarian and industrial revolutions) was certainly one of the major consequences of this intellectual and political reorientation of the west and central European élites in the course of the seventeenth century. The easy transferability of this ideal type made it an attractive model to be emulated. It offered an alternative to the impasse of crisis and ossification that bedevilled the Muscovite polity at the end of the 1680s.

To refer back to our literary conceit: Moscow was the paralysed budding hero, cameralism and the well-ordered police state had refreshed the water of the family well, and implements for drawing the water were available in the new intellectual currents of western origin and the group of foreign and native personalities trained to make use of them. Only the miracle-making pilgrims were lacking. They made their appearance in the person of Peter I. The combination of his upbringing, personality and awareness of the need to find a way out of the impasse drove Peter to reorganize brusquely and ruthlessly the political and military machinery of Muscovy along lines suggested by the 'ideal type' of the well-ordered police state (specifically borrowing from the practices of Swedish, Prussian, Dutch and other cameralist administrations). The story is well known, even though the details and motivations in individual instances still need more research. But it is absolutely clear – whatever our interpretations and judgements – that Russia was forcibly dragged into Europe by Peter; and it arrived there as an energetic and powerful giant, ready to undertake new tasks and play a big role in the affairs of Europe. It soon became obvious that there was no way back to Muscovy – not only did Peter I move the capital to newly founded St Petersburg which was rapidly rising out of the swamps of the Finnish Gulf, but he had focused the interests and curiosity of the Russian élites on to 'Europe'. The first emperor instilled the best of his subjects with the intense desire and fervent hope of becoming members, in every respect, of the European community of thought, art, literature, science and social progress. The educated in Russia, whether nobles or commoners, were never to depart from this heritage, even to this day.

In conclusion, I would like to mention an aspect which, though well known, is often not given due attention in accounting for the particular nature of the process of Russia's Europeanization in the eighteenth century. It should be emphasized that the overwhelming

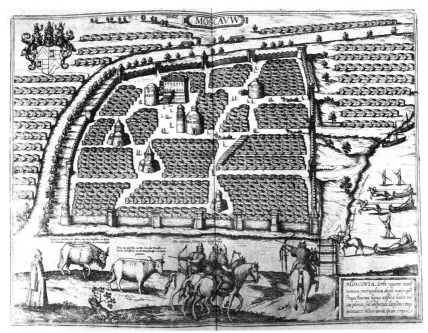

*A*n aerial view of Moscow, from the 1570 edition of Civitates
Orbis Terrarum.

majority of the foreigners – both before and during Peter's reign –
who contributed to the reorientation came from the northern, Protestant parts of Europe. Catholic and western Europe played little part
in the early stages of Russia's Europeanization. This meant that Russia
became acquainted with the Cartesian-Leibnizian rationalist tradition
rather than with the Newtonian-Lockean empirical one. It was the
German *Aufklärung*, not the Anglo-French Enlightenment, that came
to Russia in the first half of the eighteenth century. The *Aufklärung*
derived its inspiration not only from the rationalism of Descartes and
Leibniz, but also from the emotionalism of Protestant Pietism; its
interpretation of Natural Law stressed the duties and responsibilities
of the individual rather than his rights, and always viewed him as an
inseparable part and parcel of a community to which he should owe
his primary allegiance. Last, but not least, the *Aufklärung* did not
oppose religion and the Church (although it was at times critical of
particular practices) and it readily acquiesced in the authority of the
monarch or the secular powers.

This circumstance helps to explain the development of science in
Russia, the religious-moralistic tone of the intelligentsia, the absence
of doctrines of individual rights and codified legal guarantees. It also
accounts for the revival of spiritual religiosity and the enthusiastic

reception of romanticism and idealist philosophy on the part of the élites in the late eighteenth and early nineteenth century. In a sense, both Russia's academic tradition and the philosophic inspiration of the educated and of the intelligentsia have their roots in the heritage of seventeenth-century Pietism and *Naturphilosophie* mediated through the 'Rosicrucian Enlightenment' and the *Aufklärung*.

It should also be rememberd that the European scholars and technicians who came to Russia to promote its Europeanization did not belong to the avant-garde of western scientific and cultural achievements. Rather they were the 'second stringers' who had not succeeded in making a career in the West and were therefore willing to accept Peter's enticement to come to far-away and 'barbarous' Russia. What they brought, therefore, was not the most advanced knowledge and understanding, not the seminally dynamic ideas that were beginning to have their impact in western Europe, but rather the routine knowledge of their own student days. In short, in the early eighteenth century they brought not the *contemporary* culture of the West but rather the cultural achievements of the seventeenth century, particularly in their German garb.

This produced a *décalage*, a discrepancy of at least one generation, between the newly 'westernized' Russian élite and the contemporary intellectual leadership of Europe. This fact changed the dynamics and specifics of Russia's acquisition of western ideas and knowledge. When, for example, the ideas of the French Enlightenment began to penetrate into Russia in the second half of the eighteenth century, they were transformed in the process of their assimilation by Russians who were steeped in the notions of the *Aufklärung*. For this reason, too, the Russian Enlightenment always had a strong emotional, ethical and spiritual or religious component, so that its impact was to produce different conceptions of individualism, rights, law and of the role of the spiritual and of authority, a greater concern for the community and for social solidarity – all traits we note in the classics of Russian social and political thought in the late eighteenth and nineteenth centuries.

Quite obviously, this phenomenon of chronological *décalage* is an important feature in the process of cultural transfer and very relevant for the relationship between the so-called Third World and the modern West or the Soviet Union. In this sense, the history of the Europeanization of Russia may be considered a paradigm for the process of all cultural transfer.

Be that as it may, Russia's arrival in Europe in the reign of Peter the Great was not only relatively sudden, unforeseen and dramatic – it gave rise to panic and to an uneasy sense of expectation of its future role, as A. Lortholary has so well shown in his classic *Le mirage russe en France au 18e siècle* (Paris, 1951). The epic hero had been well cured! As a terrified Karl Marx had pointed out, the eighteenth century was the

The strel'tsy *mutiny of 1682 which threatened Peter the Great's position as tsar.*

'*The mice burying the cat*' – *this cartoon published on Peter the Great's death possibly reflects the conservative backlash from the 'Old Believers' and other groups which had suffered from Peter's programme of Europeanization.*

period of Russia's most dynamic expansion, an expansion no longer directed to the East and South-East but to the West and South-West: Peter I acquired the Baltic provinces, Elizabeth expanded her hold on the Ukraine, Catherine II secured the northern littoral of the Black Sea, began to encroach on the Caucasus, and, as a result of the three partitions of Poland, she brought Russia's territorial boundaries into direct contact with Austria and Prussia – and that was not to be the end of it yet. Quite clearly, this expansion would not have been possible without the institutional machinery for which Peter I had laid the groundwork by importing the methods and organization of the European well-ordered police state as well as the intellectual baggage of the *Aufklärung*.

CHAPTER VI

Russia's Rise as a European Power, 1650–1750

JEREMY BLACK

Whilst the western European powers founded great trading and colonial empires in the early-modern period, the states of central and eastern Europe were involved in a bitter fight for survival. The struggle between European society and the powers to the east has been a major theme in the history of the last millennium. The century between 1650 and 1750 was a crucial one in this struggle. It saw the definitive stemming of the Ottoman tide, and the establishment of Russian hegemony in eastern Europe. By altering the political situation in eastern Europe, the Russian victory served to change the nature of the European international system. The consequences of this success are still with us today.

The tremendous natural resources of Russia, not least its population and its size, have tended to lead to the assumption that Russian success was inevitable. This is most clearly seen in the discussion of Russo-Swedish relations. For Peter the Great it was essential to defeat Charles XII of Sweden and to conquer Sweden's possessions on the eastern shore of the Baltic – Livonia, Estonia, Ingria – if he was to achieve his ambition of linking Russia to European developments. Peter's reign was dominated by the Great Northern War with Sweden (1700–21) and it is therefore understandable that this struggle between Russia and Sweden should be seen as the pivotal war that determined Russian success. Sweden was so much poorer than Russia and its resources in people so much less, that it is easy to understand why many assume that the Swedish Empire was doomed, its defeat by Peter inevitable.

This analysis is doubtful for several reasons. The very concept of inevitability is open to question, and the determinism used to dismiss the fate of the Swedish Empire is worrying. Indeed the alacrity with which historians have used the concept of 'decline' to categorize several states in this period is unhelpful. Whatever its socio-economic fortunes, Spain, a country we are firmly told had had it, was still the largest empire in the world in 1700, as in 1800. Indeed the Spanish and Ottoman Empires took longer to disintegrate than the British Empire took to rise and fall. The

T sarevich Dmitry, a portrayal from the Grand State Book, 1672.

Swedish Empire was never in the same class as its Spanish and Ottoman counterparts, but similar caution is required in discussing its fate. It is easy to forget that in this period the gap, in terms of military strength, between the largest and the second-rank powers was much narrower than it was to become by the end of the eighteenth century. Furthermore, the challenge that the Swedes posed to Russia can only be understood by considering the general problem facing Russia: the interrelationship of three powerful enemies – Sweden, Poland-Lithuania and the Ottoman Empire. The struggle with Sweden can then be placed in perspective and the inevitability of Russian victory over her rivals questioned.

In the sixteenth century it was Poland-Lithuania that had blocked the Russian attempt to win a 'window on the West', a Baltic coastline. The disintegration of control there by the Teutonic Order led Ivan the Terrible to invade Livonia. Ivan also claimed that his state, as the 'Third Rome', was the only Orthodox state after the fall of Constantinople; as the successor to Russian rulers of the past, he himself was entitled to gather in all the 'Russian lands'. He demanded the return of Kiev, Volhynia and Podolia 'the patrimony of his forebear St Vladimir' from Poland. A vicious conflict between the two powers left Stephen Bathory of Poland victorious; the Peace of Yam Zapolski of 1582 recognized Polish control of Livonia. Poland clearly remained in the ascendancy for another half-century. In 1569 the Grand Duchy of Lithuania and the Kingdom of Poland, both ruled by one man, Sigismund-Augustus, were united by the Act of Union. His nephew Sigismund III (Sigismund Vasa) was also King of Sweden from 1592 until his deposition in 1599. In the 1620s Sigismund lost Livonia, but not to the Russians; instead it fell to the Swedes under Gustavus Adolphus, who had also sought to benefit from the collapse of the Teutonic Order.

The Russians, under the first of the Romanovs, Mikhail (1613–45), took a while to recover from the Time of Troubles, the period of protracted disorder, and contested rulership that had followed the death of Ivan. During this period Polish pretenders, in league with Russian aristocrats, claimed the throne. One such was crowned in Moscow in 1605. After his death, Sigismund III sent an army into Russia which defeated the Russians and occupied Moscow in 1610. The Polish garrison capitulated in 1612, but the Truce of Deulino (1619) left Poland with the powerful fortress of Smolensk. This Polish success, combined with the Turkish preoccupation with Persia in the first half of the century, ensured that the Polish problem was the central one for Michael and his son Alexis. In 1632 Mikhail declared war and besieged Smolensk. His failure led to the Eternal Treaty of Polianovka in 1634.

Alexis has never received the attention lavished on his son Peter the Great, but he prepared the way for many of the domestic reforms of the latter and prefigured him in his vigorous foreign policy. Poland was the central problem for Alexis. In 1654 he took the Dnieper Cossacks under his protection and moved his troops into the Ukraine, part of the Polish state. Alexis set out to conquer Belorussia, but victory led him to expand his objectives.

In 1654 Smolensk fell and the following year Alexis set out to seize the whole of Lithuania. Vilna, Minsk, Grodno and Mogilev fell and Alexis offered protection to Danzig (Gdansk). Another army invaded Galicia and threatened Lvov. In 1655 Alexis changed his title to reflect Russian control of Lithuania, Belorussia, Volhynia and Podolia. There was a strong religious element in the conflict, a factor always present in the struggle between Orthodox Russians and Catholic Poles. Russian troops were sprinkled with holy water and fought under holy banners, Orthodox churches were built in captured towns, Catholics and Jews were slaughtered in atrocities, and officers were ordered by Alexis to take communion on campaign.

In 1656 Alexis persuaded the Poles, who had also been invaded by the Swedes in 1655, to agree that he would become the next King of Poland, an elective monarchy. He had however overreached himself. The Russian declaration of war on Sweden in 1656 proved a mistake. The siege that year of the Swedish port of Riga was a failure and in 1658, faced with Polish and Tartar attacks and trouble in the Ukraine, Alexis abandoned his hopes of a Baltic seaport and signed a truce with Sweden. It also became clear that the Polish throne, a perennial target for the Russians under Alexis, would elude him.

Alexis' success had owed something to his reorganization of the Russian armed forces, a move that prefigured that of Peter, but it also owed much to the variety of enemies attacking Poland. The Russian victory in Lithuania was helped by the support received from many Lithuanian magnates opposed to royal authority. In 1654 at Perejaslaw the Cossacks under Bogdan Chmielnicki, who had rebelled against Poland in the winter of 1647–8, brought the Ukraine into the Russian Empire's sphere of influence. Charles X of Sweden, who occupied Warsaw and Cracow in 1655, the Great Elector of Brandenburg-Prussia who invaded Poland the same year, and George Rakoczi, Prince of Transylvania, who in 1657 helped to divert Polish attention from the less immediate Russian threat.

The Peace of Oliva of 1660 ended Poland's conflict with Sweden and enabled the Poles to concentrate their efforts against Russia. Their achievements suggest that it is wrong to write off the Polish state as one inevitably bound to lose out due to its aristocratic and quasi-federalist political structure, one judged anarchic by the apologists of absolutism. Just as historians have reassessed lately the vitality of the German political system – the Holy Roman Empire with its strong federalist element – so it is clear that Poland's strength in the seventeenth century can be appreciated by those who are not dominated by the hindsight of future collapse and the prejudice of believing that only 'absolutist' states would succeed.

In 1657 the Cossacks, concerned about Alexis' policies, sought to rejoin Poland as an autonomous duchy. In 1659 and 1660 the Russians were heavily defeated in the Ukraine and in 1661 they lost major towns to the Poles. In January 1664, in a winter campaign, John Casimir, King of Poland, (1648–68) invaded the eastern Ukraine, in alliance with the Tartars, the Ottoman vassals who lived in the Crimea. He was turned back, not by Alexis, but by a rising of Polish nobles under Jerzy Lubomirski, who feared the growth of royal power. As a result, the Thirteen Years' War ended in 1667 with

A royal counsellor: The boyar Ordyn-Naschokin, who as Alexis' foreign adviser in 1663 proposed a union with the Poles in a 'holy war' against the Turks.

the Truce of Andrusovo. This thirteen-year truce awarded Smolensk to Russia and partitioned the Ukraine, the left bank of the Dnieper going to Russia. This was a considerable achievement, but in no way the peace hoped for in 1654–6.

There was no sign in the 1660s that Poland was to become a Russian satellite, as it was to be a half-century later. A realization of Polish strength explains Russian interest in co-operation. The basis of this was an awareness of a common threat from Sweden and Turkey. In 1583 Bathory had proposed to Ivan IV joint action against the Turks; the following year he had considered a federation with Russia. In 1663, Alexis' adviser, Afanasy Ordyn-Nashchokin, proposed a union with the Poles and a war against the Turks. He suggested that the Poles could serve as a link with the Christians of Moldavia and Wallachia (modern Rumania) and that the latter could be persuaded to rise against the Turks. Six years later Robert Yard, a British observer in Moscow, reported that the Russians were pleased with the election of John Casimir's successor, Michael Korybut (1669–73), as the latter was ready to negotiate an anti-Turkish alliance:

> . . . the Muscovites interest is to have a firm peace with that crown [Poland] for the effecting of which they labour hard, and which being concluded they will think themselves sufficiently able to grapple with all other enemys whatsoever.

The same year Peter Wych reported from Moscow that a Russia at peace with Poland 'will slight all other attempts . . . The Polish Envoy may be here today or tomorrow, for whom these people always lay aside all other business.' Alongside this interest in better relations, an interest that was to lead Alexis to try to gain the Polish throne after the death of Michael Korybut, was an awareness of continued tension. Yard noted the belief in Moscow that the Poles would never quit their claims to Kiev and Smolensk.

The balance was to be tilted towards co-operation by Turkish action. A series of semi-autonomous Turkish buffer-states – Transylvania, Wallachia, Moldavia, Tartary – had absorbed tension between the Ottoman Empire and its northern neighbours. The Ukrainian rebellion and the consequent increase of Russian influence destroyed the regional balance of power and created in the Ukraine a vortex that drew in the great powers, helping to ensure that from the late 1650s until 1700 Russian foreign policy was dominated by the problem of the south. In the 1660s Hetman Doroshenko of the Ukraine became a Turkish vassal and strove to put all the Ukraine under Turkish protection. In 1672 Sultan Muhammad IV led a Turkish invasion of the Polish province of Podolia. The important fortress of Kamieniec Podolski was captured, its cathedral turned into a mosque and King Michael forced to recognize Turkish suzerainty over the western Ukraine and to agree to pay a heavy annual tribute to the Sultan. Alexis' conduct was not that of a ruler who dominated the situation; instead he sought to create a European coalition against the Turks. However, he failed and left the task of fighting the Turks in the early 1670s to the Poles under Sobieski (1674–96).

The Russian stance in the 1670s was not an aggressive one. In 1673 Alexis pressed for free trading rights at the Swedish Baltic points of Riga and Reval, but there was no wish to fight the Swedes. In 1677 the British envoy John Hebdon reported that the new Tsar, Alexis' oldest surviving son, Feodor II, wanted peace with Sweden 'being at present threatened on all sides not alone by the Pole but also by the Turk and Tartar'. The Danes pressed the Russians to attack the Swedes and urged them to gain a foothold on the Baltic, but without success, Hebdon commenting, 'The Russes know they could do nothing against the Swedes when they had 100,000 men.'

Russian attention continued to be directed to the south, the Ukraine. Aside from Turkish interest, it was also feared that the Poles, who regarded the 1667 agreement as only a temporary one, would seek to regain left-bank Ukraine. However, it was the Turks who proved the major threat. Having signed a truce with the Poles in 1676, a Turkish army invaded the Ukraine the following year and besieged Kiev without success.

The strain of the conflict in the late 1670s, combined with caution in committing Russian forces to a new European alliance, account for the Russian delay in joining the new war touched off by the Turkish march on Vienna in 1683. Sobieski played a major role in the relief of besieged Vienna and in the campaigns that followed it. The Austrians overran Hungary; Sobieski planned to conquer Moldavia. The prospect of a fundamental shift in the balance of power in favour of Poland and Austria helped to lead Russia to join the anti-Turkish camp. In 1686 the Russians and Poles signed a Treaty of Eternal Peace. This confirmation of the terms of Andrusovo made permanent the Russian gain of Kiev and left-bank Ukraine. The Polish envoy was subsequently accused of having exceeded his instructions, but the Poles were not in a position to challenge it. As part of the treaty, Russia agreed to launch a war against the Crimean Tartars.

This represented a substantial southward extension of Russian activity. In 1642 a Cossack offer of the port of Azov, the important Turkish base on the Sea of Azov (which leads to the Black Sea) that had been captured the previous year, had had to be declined by the Russians who felt unable to risk war for it. In 1687 and 1689, however, Russian armies under Prince Golitsyn, the lover and chief minister of Alexis' daughter Sophia (regent 1682–9) invaded the Crimea. The failure of the campaigns helped to ensure the success of Peter the Great's challenge to Sophia's authority in 1689. After a lull in the early 1690s, the Russians, led by Peter, besieged Azov in

1695. A lengthy siege failed, partly because of the ability of the Turks, a major naval power, to reinforce Azov by sea. Peter returned the following year, and, as his father had done, built a navy on the River Don. With the help of this he was able to take Azov. Peter's plans were not restricted to Azov. He ordered the construction of a major naval base nearby at Taganrog. In 1697 Peter signed a treaty with Austria and Venice, both then at war with the Turks, under which the powers agreed to continue the war until the Turks consented to cede to Russia the port of Kerch, which controlled the passage between the Sea of Azov and the Black Sea. Peter clearly aimed to establish Russian power on the northern shores of the Black Sea. In 1695 a Russian army had captured the Turkish forts at the north of the Dnieper. The entrances to the Balkans were being cleared.

Peter was ditched by his allies. At the peace congress at Carlowitz in 1699 Russian demands for Kerch were ignored and all Peter gained was a two-year truce with the Turks. This was converted into a treaty the following year. Russian gains were little better than those of Poland and compared neither to Austria-Hungary, nor to Venice – in southern Greece. Russia suffered from its failures in the late 1680s and inaction in the early 1690s, but also from its lack of diplomatic clout.

It is difficult to say what would have happened to Russian foreign policy had the war with Turkey continued. Peter's epic personal struggle with Charles XII of Sweden has tended to divert attention from his great interest in his southern frontiers, an interest that was to lead him to invade Moldavia in person in 1711 and to campaign in Transcaucasia and Persia in the last years of his reign. The lure of Constantinople was to be a major theme in eighteenth-century Russian foreign policy, one that owed much to a semi-mystical vision of Russia's role that drew both on the theme of the Third Rome and on the idea of Russia as a Christian crusading power that would free the Balkans. Alongside the view of eighteenth-century international relations as 'rational', governed by sober considerations of *raison d'état*, it is necessary to consider other forces at work. Just as Protestants still feared alliances between Catholic powers, and Frederick the Great sought to challenge the Habsburg-Catholic ascendancy in central Europe, so many Russians hoped to free their Orthodox brethren in the Balkans. Russia would naturally benefit from such a development. Alexis had been opposed to leaving the western Ukraine with Poland, both because he did not like to see his co-religionists under Catholic rule and because he wanted Russia to dominate the Ukraine. In the same manner, Peter hoped that the spread of Orthodox influence into the Balkans would weaken both Poland and the Ottoman Empire.

Russia was most vulnerable when confronted by an alliance of her neighbours and it was this that made the Great Northern War so dangerous. Initially, it began under propitious circumstances for

A royal counsellor: Prince Golitsyn, adviser and possibly lover of Alexis' daughter, the Regent Sophia. The failure of his Crimean campaigns of 1687–9 paved the way for Peter the Great to assume complete power.

Russia. An alliance with Frederick IV of Denmark and Augustus II, Elector of Saxony and King of Poland, offered a good opportunity to defeat the isolated Swedish Empire. The envisaged Russian role was a limited one; compared to the great prospects that war against the Turks had offered, the Great Northern War in its opening stages offered far less. In particular, Augustus appeared to benefit, being allocated the promise of Livonia and hoping that victory against

Sweden would enable him to increase royal authority in Poland.
A more effective Poland was not a welcome prospect for Russia.
Polish interests in Moldavia challenged Russian aspirations, dissi-
dent elements in left-bank Ukraine would be able to seek Polish
support. Thus, the diplomatic developments of 1699–1700, although
they offered Peter the opportunity of gaining Ingria and a 'window
on the Baltic', also revealed the limited role allocated to Russia in
the international system. Charles XII's military skill destroyed the
diplomatic house of cards. In 1700 Denmark was knocked out of the
war and the Russian forces under Peter were defeated at Narva.

However, Charles did not follow up by an advance into Russia.
Instead, he turned south, invading Poland (1701). Augustus was de-
feated and the protégé of Charles, Stanislaus Leszcynski, was elected
King. The creation of a Swedish-Polish bloc represented a major
threat to Peter that was far more serious than the challenge posed by
Swedish control of the Baltic provinces. From 1701 Polish 'patriots',

*R*ussia under Peter the Great.

such as the commander of the army, Jablonowski, pressed for co-operation with Charles in order to regain the lands lost to Russia in 1667, lands which succeeding kings of Poland on their election had sworn to reconquer. In the Swedish-Polish treaty of 1705 Charles promised to help reconquer these lands. In 1696–7 the Russians had opposed the candidature of a Frenchman, the Prince de Conti, for the Polish throne, because they feared he would be anti-Russian. The election of Stanislaus was far more serious: it threatened the fragile territorial stability of Russia's western and southern border. Furthermore, it opened up the possibility of an alliance between Sweden, Poland and the Turks. In 1699 Charles XII had not only pressed Augustus II on their supposed common interests against Russia. He had encouraged the Turks to continue their war with Russia.

It was fortunate for Peter that in the 1700s the Turks sought to avoid conflict with him, ignoring pleas for assistance from the Tartars and the opportunity for intervention provided by the unpopularity of Peter's policies in the Ukraine. Furthermore, Charles, busy seeking to establish Stanislaus in the quagmire of Polish politics, was not free to attack Russia until 1708. However, the conflicting interests of the two powers in Poland made peace between them impossible. Peter was fighting, not only for his 'window on the west', for which St Petersburg had been founded on the Gulf of Finland in 1703, but also to prevent Poland from becoming a Swedish client state. Peter sent money and troops to the aid of Polish nobles opposed to Charles; in 1707 he supported the candidature for the Polish throne of the Hungarian leader Rakoczi. A Swedish invasion of Russia seemed the only way to end the interminable Polish civil war.

Charles XII's defeat by the Russians at Poltava in the Ukraine in 1709 solved both the Polish question and that of the Baltic provinces. Poltava led to the effective end of the Swedish party in Poland. Leszcynski fled to the Swedish base at Stettin, Augustus II was restored in 1710. In the same year, Russian troops overran Sweden's eastern Baltic provinces, bar Finland, seizing Viborg, Reval and Riga. Russian possession of the Baltic provinces was not to be seriously challenged until Napoleon. At this moment of triumph Peter badly miscalculated. Charles XII had fled to Bender in the Ottoman Empire after Poltava and he worked hard to provoke a war between the Turks and the Russians. Peter's determination to treat the Ukraine as Russian, rather than as the buffer territory that the Turks wanted it to be, was exploited by the anti-Russian party in Constantinople. In November 1710, the Turks declared war. Russian agents were sent to the Balkans to organize risings, proclamations were issued urging the Balkan Christians to revolt, and, in conscious imitation of Constantine the Great, Peter had the cross inscribed on his standards with the motto 'Under this sign we conquer'. In April 1711, the Hospodar of Moldavia, Demetrius Cantemir, signed a treaty with Peter agreeing to support him in return for acknowledgement as hereditary Prince of Moldavia under Russian protection. Peter planned to cross the Danube, but supply problems and the speedy movement of a large Turkish army led to the Russian army being surrounded in July at the River Pruth and forced to ask for terms.

Peter was willing to abandon Livonia and Azov and recognize Leszcynski as King of Poland, but the Turkish terms were moderate. He had to agree to return Azov, to destroy Taganrog and his new Dnieper fortress and to promise not to interfere in Polish affairs. Peter's unwillingness to implement the peace terms led to disputes with the Turks that continued until 1713. However, Peter was forced to accept the loss of Azov and of Russian naval power on the Black Sea; not until the Treaty of Kuchuk-Kainardji of 1774 was Russia allowed to fortify Azov.

Peter's failure to gain 'a window on the Black Sea' and to become the dominant power in the eastern Balkans contrasted with his success in the Baltic. The former has never received the attention it deserved. It is difficult to speculate as to what the consequences of Russian success would have been. Had the Turkish Empire suffered serious defeat, a power vacuum might have been created in the Balkans and in Transcaucasia that would have sucked the Russians in, rather as they were sucked into Persian politics in

A medal struck to commemorate the 'eternal peace' of 1686, showing Jan Sobieski, 'the Polish hammer of the Turks' and hero of the relief of Vienna.

the early 1720s by the collapse of the Safavid Dynasty. As it was, the continued vitality of the Turkish Empire served to thwart Peter, just as logistical problems and the victories of Nadir Shah were to end Russian occupation of the southern shores of the Caspian in the early 1730s.

Although Peter failed to achieve his aims on his southern frontiers, he had more success in establishing himself as a European power. This was symbolized by the development of marital links with a number of German princely families reflecting Peter's prestige and helping to ensure his close involvement in German politics. The latter was also made necessary by the resilience of Charles XII, who in 1714 left Bender and resumed his attempts to defend the Swedish Empire. In response, Peter moved his troops westward. In 1716 he prepared to invade southern Sweden from Denmark and that winter quartered his troops on the German Baltic coast in Mecklenburg. This assertive stance led to divisions among the powers who had attacked Sweden after Poltava: Denmark, Hanover and Prussia. It was generally feared that the European system was threatened by Russian preponderance, and individual rulers, such as George I of Hanover-Britain, had particular quarrels with Peter. Other rulers, exhausted by the Spanish Succession and Northern Wars, were both astonished and frightened by Peter's ability to go on fielding large forces. In December 1716, Lord Polwarth, the British envoy in Copenhagen, wrote:

Relief side of the medal struck to celebrate the 'eternal peace' of 1686 between Russia and Poland showing the two nations in harmony.

The Czar makes a very formidable figure in these parts. He has above 35,000 men in Mecklenburg, 30,000 in Poland who are demanding winter quarters in Polish Prussia, a fleet of above twenty ships of the line, and galleys in which he can transport above 50,000 men, and withall one of the best ports in the Baltic, as he has made it, at Reval. It were to be wished that a peace in these parts might give his Majesty leisure to turn so considerable a force towards his frontiers on the other side, as he so earnestly wishes.

Two months earlier, another British diplomat, Charles Whitworth, confessed his fears about Peter's schemes, adding:

The great facility he has hitherto met in all his pretentions may indeed encourage him to very wild undertakings, and in such may quite unravel the scheme which has been so long laying in the North; but all circumstances considered, if the proper measures be taken, and the Prussian court will but come tolerably into their own interests, they must at last end as much to his confusion as the enterprise on the Pruth did.

George I, concerned about Russian intervention in the neighbouring Duchy of Mecklenburg, in whose domestic politics he was greatly interested, played the leading role in negotiating peace between Sweden and her western enemies, and in creating a powerful anti-Russian coalition. British diplomatic pressure played a major role in Peter's withdrawal from Mecklenburg in 1717. The following year, the British tried to bribe the Turks to attack Russia. In January 1719, Austria, Hanover and Saxony signed a treaty aimed at driving Russian troops out of Poland. In November 1719, Augustus II's minister, Count Flemming, told George I that the Poles would fight Russia if they were promised Kiev and Smolensk, and a large subsidy. George agreed. British squadrons were sent to the eastern Baltic to attack the Russian fleet and in February 1720 George I signed an alliance with Sweden, promising support for Swedish demands for the return of the Baltic provinces. Thus, by 1720 Peter faced the prospect of a major war with a powerful European coalition which, however, was less of a threat than that posed by Charles XII in 1709–10. His opponents were divided and weary after many years of war. Despite their British alliance, the French and the Dutch did not want to fight. The Austrians were more concerned about Italy, the Prussians fearful of Russia, the Poles unwilling to fight. George I faced domestic opposition to war, and, his ministry endangered by the South Sea Bubble, was forced to abandon his anti-Russian plans. Deserted by her allies, Sweden signed the peace of Nystad in August 1721, and ceded her eastern Baltic provinces to Peter.

The disintegration of the anti-Russian coalition in 1720 and the failure of the British attempt to create a *barrière de l'est* against Russia was both cause and effect of Peter's triumph. In diplomatic terms this was sealed at Nystad and reflected by the frantic effort of the European powers to win Russian support in 1725–6 during the confrontation between the alliances of Hanover and Vienna. Peter had solved both the Polish and the Swedish problems. It was the interrelationship between his successes that was crucial. Had Poland been a powerful active force in 1709, then Poltava would have been less crucial; a decade later she might have made the anti-Russian schemes a reality. It was Polish weakness that was crucial both to Peter's conquest of Sweden's eastern Baltic provinces and to his retention of them, just as it permitted Russia to dominate the Ukraine. An awareness of this helps to account for Russia's determination to retain influence in Poland. Control of Poland was central to eighteenth-century Russia's diplomatic and military strategies. Because of it, plans to challenge Russia's control of her borderlands, such as those floated in Sweden in 1727 for an invasion of her former Baltic provinces, stood little chance of success. Helped by her preponderant international position in eastern Europe, Russia was able partially to integrate her Baltic and Ukrainian conquests into her dominions. Russia's victories in her wars in Poland (1733–5) and against Sweden (1741–3) and her avoidance of a defeat against the Turks (1736–9) enabled Peter's successors to consolidate his triumphs. However, it was not until Catherine the Great and the Russo-Turkish war of 1768–74 (a war in which Polish events were again of great importance), that some of his southern schemes were realized. Securely in control of her borderlands, Russia was able to intervene with greater weight in European affairs. For example, the Russian march towards the Rhine in 1735 helped to persuade France to end her conflict with Austria. The century 1650–1750 witnessed the creation of Russian hegemony in eastern Europe. It is only now disintegrating.

CHAPTER VII

On Crime and Punishment

MAX J. OKENFUSS

I n Captain John Perry's *State of Russia under the Present Czar* (London, 1716), the English naval engineer and canal builder echoed old themes when he discoursed upon the rampant immorality of the Russians. Their clergy, he reported, could not and did not preach sermons, could not debate theology, and more important, the pardons they granted to the sinful seldom had the effect of correcting even the most outrageous misbehaviour:

> The doing some short Penance for Sins past, when enjoin'd; and the asking Forgiveness of the Priest, which when he has cross'd them and pronounc'd their Pardon, they go away as well satisfied as if they had never done any harm, though they had committed the most detestable Crimes in the World.

Perry's principal conclusions are unmistakable. The Russians were shameless liars and deceivers, their solemn oaths were worthless, and neither the religion of the Church nor the physical chastisement of the State reformed them one whit.

For John Perry the latter point was integrally linked to the first:

> Another Reason that may be alledg'd for the *Russes* having the want of the sense of Shame and Scandal for any the most wicked Things, is, that after their being beat with the *Batoags* or *Knout*, tho' done by the Hands of a common Hangman, there is no mark of Infamy set upon them for it; there is nothing more ordinary in *Russia* than to have them afterwards be again admitted into Places of Honour and Trust.

Perry described in vivid, gory detail both the beatings with batogs, and the two different but equally brutal manners of flailing with the knout, but his point was that those who survived such cruelty 'never blush for the Roguery they have committed', but rather accepted punishment as inevitable, as an evidence of God's or the tsar's displeasure, but it did not entail the mending of one's ways. In short, the accused Russian stood alone, accepted civil or ecclesiastical punishment, and neither Church penance nor civil knout effected repentance: his sense of morality was thoroughly debased.

Such judgements were a commonplace in the travel literature of Russia in early-modern times, and foreigners agreed that the Russians followed a very strange moral light. Indeed, as early as the sixteenth

*L*ivonian peasantry being punished with the batog. From Olearius's
Voyages.

century, Giles Fletcher even concluded that their corrupt sense of
morality was encouraged by a conscious governmental policy; firstly,
the State supported a corrupt Church, 'knowing superstition and a
false religion best to agree with a tyrannical state', and secondly, it
supported a regime of base servility, since a world of cruelty:

> . . . void of all good learning and civil behaviour – is thought by their
> governors most agreeable to that state and their manner of government,
> which the people would hardly bear if they were once civilled and brought
> to more understanding of God and good policy.

The result of tyrannical government, corrupt religion and a regime
of senseless wanton brutality was a people who knew only deceit and
guile, who thought neither of repentance nor redemption, but only of
amoral survival, and a people whose Church neither comforted nor
corrected, nor cared to.

Now obviously this unflattering portrait is exaggerated and overdrawn. Doubtless many found both consolation and solid moral
example from the Orthodox clergy, a clergy capable of periodic
self-regeneration in early-modern times. An important moral guide

from sixteenth-century Muscovy, the *Domostroi*, described a thoroughly ethical realm in which the humble village clergy served as teachers in schools-without-walls, in which their pupils, the heads of households, transmitted clear rules of daily behaviour to those entrusted to their care. For the recalcitrant child, servant or mate, the rod of correction was recommended, but *Domostroi* endeavoured to regulate all potentially sinful personal and social relationships. It set very high moral standards indeed, certainly not inferior to those of contemporary western Europe.

There is, however, evidence that somewhere and somehow between the sixteenth and the late eighteenth centuries, something dramatic occurred in the realm of Russian public morality. Thoroughly despicable governors and landowners are found in Alexander Radishchev's *Journey from Petersburgh to Moscow* (1790), but a moral and humane Radishchev was there to condemn them, and to urge his readers to do likewise. Isabel de Madariaga has recently and brilliantly surveyed the previous half-century of moral reform – Catherine the Great's own didactic *Nakaz* based on Montesquieu's and Beccaria's notions of Enlightened law, her reform and re-education of the clergy

*M*orality and manners. Religious devotion – kissing the icon.

in the age of the Enlightenment, her new system of justice based on the English court of equity, her encouragement of a moralizing periodical press modelled on the *Spectator* and *Tatler* – all attest to the fact that the westernizing process in Russia was also a process of moral reformation.

While the conclusion of this process can be seen in the Russia of Catherine the Great, the question arises, At what point did Russians become aware of a moral divide between traditional Muscovy and the Christian West? Can we document a perception on the part of ordinary Russians, when they began to appreciate the fact that Christianity meant something very different in the West, Protestant or Catholic, than it did in Orthodox Muscovy? One early bit of evidence is to be found in the travel diary of Count Peter Tolstoi, a middle-aged courtier who was sent (along with scores of others), to western Europe for specialized technical training when Peter the Great commenced his active rule of Russia in the last years of the seventeenth century. Usually read for Tolstoi's observations on European art and architecture, the diary in fact chronicles the moral awakening of a Russian servitor, and anticipates the ethical re-education of a nation over the next hundred years.

On 5 July 1698, Peter Tolstoi, for example, was invited to witness the public execution of a murderer on the piazza in front of the Spanish Viceroy's palace in Naples. Tolstoi's ghastly account of breaking on the wheel rivals in graphic detail European reporting of Peter the Great's execution of the rebellious *strel'tsy* (the musketeers) at home in Moscow just three months later. But if the pedagogy of public execution was similar, there was also a moral difference.

Tolstoi went out of his way to note repeatedly the ministrations of the Neapolitan clergy, a feature routinely absent in foreigners' tales of executions in Moscow. 'Alongside the condemned man, who carried a crucifix, walked two priests of the Roman faith . . ., and one was his spiritual father, [who] talked with him constantly, in order that he might mention his sins and be in the hope of salvation, and not fall into despair.' His confessor 'whispered in his ear for a quarter of an hour, so he would not despair of the mercy of God'. Bound to the wheel, the victim was yet accompanied by his confessor, who 'sat on the wheel over him with the cross and unceasingly strengthened him with words, so that he was not frightened of death'. After the execution, the collected clergy 'kneeled on the ground around the wheel and prayed for the soul of the condemned man, that God might forgive him his sins'. Although his body was quartered and strewn on the fields, presumably his soul fared better, thanks to the ministry of the Catholic clergy. The extended commentary in the diary strongly suggests that Tolstoi that day witnessed a role played by the Catholic priests which he had not observed among the Orthodox clergy at home.

At other times and in various places Tolstoi noted, in addition to the role of the confessor, the other pastoral roles of the western clergy. In Naples he visited a hospital where 'every day six priests take turns attending to the spiritual needs of the sick'. With a full complement of pharmacists and doctors, the hospital's staff 'cure all the sick and give them drink and food all without cost in the name of Christ; and he who dies is buried at the Church's expense'. Repeated passages of this kind show clearly that in western Europe Tolstoi encountered a level of Christian clerical charity which did not exist in his native Muscovy, which lacked not only hospitals, but also that compassion born of their faith. In Rome he saw a papal hospital for impoverished nobles:

> Everything in the rooms of those ill in the way of food and medicine and everything else is paid by the papal treasury. And when a man of high birth, or a Roman prince, or one of a noble senatorial family falls ill, and cannot hire a doctor himself for his own lack of means, he comes to those papal hospitals.

Whether administering a pauper hospital for the well-born, or Catholic convents which nurtured orphans and prepared them for careers and marriage, the religious communities of the West were apparently devoted to a level of earthly compassion unknown in Russia. Everywhere Tolstoi noted both the work of the religious orders and parish clergy, and also their influence on the laity, seen in the charitable activities of civil Europeans, from monarchs to ordinary subjects. And everywhere he observed the impact of Christianity on daily life. In Vienna he encountered a hospital maintained by the Emperor:

> They accept into this hospital the sick of every rank without cost, and only enquire whether the sick person has no means of his own . . . When they are completely healthy, then they are free to go wherever they wish without paying; . . . they do this because of their Christian faith and for the saving of souls.

In Milan Tolstoi saw the hospital known as 'Ca' Granda', and noted that its medical care was rendered gratis, financed by donated estates and managed by volunteer 'senators'. 'In this matter one can recognize the love of mankind of the Catholics, such as one scarcely finds anywhere in the world.' In Naples he saw an insane asylum in which nobles humbly volunteered their services to tend the helpless, those who could not care for themselves, and who might otherwise be abused out in society. 'Honourable people serve the sick for the sake of Christ; many honourable people come here, cover themselves with aprons, and distribute food to the sick.' The hospital was supported by a tax levy imposed by the Spanish Viceroy, Tolstoi noted, and thus all who enter can be cared for free, 'for the sake of Christ'.

A seventeenth-century flogging, from the Palmqvist *album.*

On the island of Malta, the Grand Master's treasury supported a hospital for Christians, but one which also accepted even Muslim infidels, and 'all day long doctors and druggists come to the sick and cure them gratis'. More remarkable was the behaviour of the illustrious knights, who abased themselves and served the sick, 'for the love of Christ'. Tolstoi noted their selflessness and this humility, and made it clear that he had never observed Muscovite nobles at home in such Christian service. The diary echoes with the refrains, 'for the sake of Christ', 'for the love of Christ', and, 'they do this because of their Christian faith'; Tolstoi explicitly recognized the moral divide between his religion and that of Christian Europe.

In Catherine the Great's Russia, three-quarters of a century later, after the secularization of Church lands, the State issued a Provincial Statute, hailed by Voltaire as 'the Gospel of the universe', in which each province was ordered to establish and maintain schools, orphanages, hospitals, almshouses, lunatic asylums, workhouses and houses of correction. Other enlightened monarchs also sponsored such institutions, as their states assumed more and more of the functions previously exercised mainly by the Church. In Peter Tolstoi's diary of 1697–8, on the eve of Peter the Great's first 'westernization', one can see the first awareness by an ordinary Russian of this Christian component in the growth of the services of the modern state. In the West the transfer occurred most dramatically in the French Revolution, but elsewhere the process, if slower, was no less certain.

Tolstoi was also witness to two phenomena, one new and one ancient, but both unknown in the Orthodox Muscovy he left. First, he witnessed the birth of modern medicine and modern medical care. At home in his own lifetime medical practitioners could still be at best regarded with scepticism and mistrust, at worst charged as sorcerers, subject to the death penalty. Even before the Enlightenment in the West, modern medical practice was being born as the humane component in the rise of the scientific spirit, and by the mid-century, as Peter Gay noted, it had contributed mightily to a 'recovery of nerve', one which was everywhere visible, in faces clear of the ravages of smallpox, in the declining death rates of mothers in childbirth, and in the increasing survival rates of the newborn.

More important for our purposes, Tolstoi witnessed a uniquely western, worldly, Christian charity and moral concern on the part of clergy and laity alike. Long integral to western Christianity, it was now giving rise to a modern, secular humanism, born ironically of the incremental decline of religiosity itself. With the end of religious warfare, the simultaneous rise of modern medicine and a spirit of toleration came a new Christianity which cared equally for health, happiness and the comfort of believers in this world, and for their eternal salvation in the next.

In his private observations, Peter Tolstoi came to realize, if not to articulate, the difference between stern, old, eastern Christianity, born of Cyril of Alexander's monophysite Christology, and the West's Leonine Christology, which emphasized strongly the human nature of Christ, in its turn the ultimate source of modern humanism. The former led inevitably to a greater concern with Communion with God in the Hereafter, the latter to Christian charity on this earth. Although Peter Tolstoi returned from Europe to assist Peter the Great in Russia's political and economic transformation, the first step was the reorientation of Russian Orthodoxy itself. Within months of his own visit to Holland and England, where he discussed church affairs with Bishop Burnet of Salisbury, Tsar Peter began his 'programme for a Russian Reformation', as Georges Florovsky has termed it. Peter's hand-picked aide was Feofan Prokopovich, Rome-educated, and it was Feofan who eased Russian Orthodoxy away from its eastern traditions. When Peter imposed a new discipline and leadership on the Russian Church, when he championed Feofan's new notions of monarchy and his new catechism, it was a 'victory for Protestant scholastic theology'. 'There can be no debate or hesitation about the proper conclusion: Feofan was actually a Protestant.'

It would take a full century for this new Christianity to penetrate all levels of Russian society, but the eighteenth-century re-education of the clergy was the first step. Among the laity, it was foreshadowed by the Freemasons in Catherine's Russia, but its first mass appearance was perhaps to be found among the hundreds of young Russian army officers who had been stationed in the outskirts of Paris after the Napoleonic wars. They returned home to found secret societies 'to disseminate the true rules of morality and enlightenment among fellow citizens, and to assist the government in elevating Russia to the level of greatness and welfare to which the Creator has predestined it'. But at the dawn of Russia's modern age, Peter Tolstoi was among the first to notice the moral chasm between East and West, and to note the wonders worked by the other Christianity.

CHAPTER VIII

Peter the Great and the Modern World

L. R. LEWITTER

Leaving aside any precise definition of modernity, let us agree that a desire for improvement, a predilection for novelty, an attitude of mind that is proper to the avant-garde in any generation or epoch, were essential aspects of the *mentalité* of Peter the Great. This frame of mind also owes something to a historical conception of human society, to the belief that its changing condition and the changing condition of mankind are the result of a process which is measured by time. For the optimists the change deliberately effected by the exertions of man is one for the better: 'Today is better than yesterday and tomorrow will be better than today.' The world is knowable, describable and capable of improvement. Society can be transformed by the labour of man, of *homo faber* who is not a passive object of the revolutions of the wheel of fortune, but moves forward of his own volition on an upward path leading to a glorious future. One of the driving forces in his progress is the desire for novelty or innovation. A potent instrument of change for the better is the ruler who has the wisdom to plan, and the power to enforce reform.

These patterns of thought are characteristic also of Peter Alekseevich. His taste for novelty was remarked upon later in the century by the future Frederick the Great: '*Pierre le Grand était gouverné par des fantaisies assez nouvelles.*' Like all innovators, he was impatient and acutely aware of the ineluctable passage of time. In 1701 he wrote to the official in charge of the re-equipment of the artillery: 'Make haste, for time is like death.' A year or so earlier, in accordance with ancient custom, Muscovy had welcomed the new year on 1 September 7208, from the Creation, but late in December Tsar Peter unexpectedly decreed that the forthcoming first day of January would be celebrated as New Year's Day and the year would be numbered 1700. In doing so, he not only synchronized Russian historical time with western Europe (except for the discrepancy between the Julian and the Gregorian calendars), but also made full use of the pivotal significance of the years 1699 and 1700, the first by reason of its closeness to the number of the Beast capable of inspiring apocalyptic fears, the second marking the auspicious turning over of a new leaf. At the same time, the order went out to change the clock faces on watch-towers 'so that the hours are shown in the European manner

*P*eter the Great painted by Godfrey Kneller for William III, during
Peter's visit to Britain in 1698.

from one to twelve, that is from noon and from midnight and not (as now) from morning till evening with the figures running from one to seventeen'.

The fresh start was marked in Moscow by the celebration of a liturgy, a display of fireworks, illuminations, triumphal arches and a three-gun salute. Peter I had slammed the door on Muscovy and entered a new age. But the ground before him looked arid. In 1697 Leibniz had already spoken of Russia as a *tabula rasa, 'comme une nouvelle terre qu'on veut défricher, les moscovites n'étant pas encore parvenus en matière de science'*.

The lessons of the past, however, were not to be forgotten. The catalogue of Peter's library suggests that he took a keen interest in Byzantine history and he is known to have reflected more than once in public and in private on the fall of Byzantium, caused, as he believed, by the neglect of the use of arms by land and sea and contempt for the law. The presence in his library of several accounts of various periods in the history of Muscovy show that he was fully aware of the relevance of the Muscovite inheritance to his own day. His attitude to the most recent past, the last quarter of the seventeenth century, could only have been critical and negative, his very passion for the new signals a detestation of the old. Peter had every reason to want to suppress the memory of the successive revolts of the *strel'tsy* (and his own sinister part in the quelling of the last one), the turbulent regency of Sophia Alekseevna, the meddling in politics of the last two patriarchs and his forced marriage to Evdokiia (Eudoxia) Lopukhina, to open the trap door of oblivion under the whole dramatis personae, costumes, scenery and stifling aura eventually to be resurrected in Mussorgsky's *Khovanshchina*.

Later, from about 1713, he was to fear a relapse of the new Russia of his making into the obscurantism and stagnation of old Muscovy, a reaction presided over by his son and heir Alexis, whom he charged, before long, with hypocrisy, idleness and unwillingness to learn. But for that anxiety, he viewed the present with pride and drew comfort for the future from a belief which came close to a cyclical or migratory view of the history of civilization. According to the Hanoverian envoy, Weber, in 1719, at the launching of a man-of-war in St Petersburg, the Tsar spoke as follows:

Brethren, who is that man among you, who thirty years ago could have had even the thought of being employed with me in ship carpenter's work here in the Baltic; of coming hither in a German dress to settle in these countries conquered by our fatigues and bravery; of living to see so many brave and victorious soldiers and seamen sprung from Russian blood; to see our sons coming home able men from foreign countries; to see so many outlandish artificers and handicraftsmen settling in our dominions, and to see the remotest potentates express so great an esteem for us? The historians place the ancient seat of all sciences in Greece, from whence being expelled by the fatality of the times, they spread in Italy, and afterwards dispersed themselves all over Europe, but by the perverseness of our ancestors were hindered from penetrating any further into Poland, though the Poles as well as the Germans formerly groped in the same darkness in which we have lived hitherto, but the indefatigable care of their governors opened their eyes at length that they made themselves masters of those arts, sciences and improvements of life that formerly Greece boasted of. It is now our turn, if you will seriously second my designs, and add to your blind obedience a voluntary knowledge, and apply yourselves to the enquiry of good and evil. I can compare this transmigration of sciences with nothing better than the circulation of the blood in the human body, and my mind almost gives me [reason] to believe that they will some time or other quit their abode in England, France and Germany, and come to settle for some centuries among us, and perhaps afterwards return again to their original home in Greece. In the meantime I earnestly recommend to your practice the Latin saying, *Ora et labora*, pray and work, and in that case be persuaded, you may happen even in our lifetime to put other civilized nations to the blush, and to carry the glory of the Russian name to the highest pitch.

It is obvious that the process described by Peter is not an automatic one, that it must be kept in motion by the exertions of *homo faber*: civilization will only flourish in circumstances made favourable by man. He himself, the labourer on the throne, the *Zar und Zimmermann* who had helped to build ships with his own hands at Zaandam and in Deptford, was of that mould. A glutton for work, he branded idleness as 'the root of all evil'. Modern as this condemnation may sound, it was derived, perhaps not surprisingly, from the Byzantine tradition. Peter's private vices, of which there were many, were not of a kind to create so great a demand for goods and services that they could be accounted public virtues. His personal needs were modest in the extreme. It was said that he acquired the habit of thrift during his first stay in the Netherlands in 1697. Hand in hand with frugality went an intense dislike of the kind of ostentation and extravagance that he had occasion to observe at close quarters in Paris and at Versailles in 1717. Luxury, he predicted, would be the undoing of France – a conservative attitude for once, but a sound one. Even as a public figure, he did not consider it necessary to augment his prestige by a display of architectural grandeur, his residences were designed for living in rather than for show.

The Crown Prince of Prussia, already quoted, correctly noted Peter's willingness to be guided by a liking for novelty, but misunderstood his motives which went far beyond a desire to impress – '*pour donner un certain éclat, pour éblouir*'. The attraction to novelty led him in 1697–8 to his particular dreamland prosaically located in southern England and in Holland. Here he could see men as God-fearing as they were materialistic, engaged in vigorous enterprise, capitalists growing rich on the fruits of seaborne trade and native manufacture, a flourishing urban civilization supported by geographical discovery, technical invention and the skilful handling of money.

In order to rise to the same degree of power and wealth, it was necessary to gain access to the trade routes of the world and it was in pursuit of this aim that Peter I, having already begun the intermittent war with Turkey, became involved in the Great Northern War against Sweden (1700–21) and finally invaded Persia (1722–3). No foothold could be established on the Sea of Azov, let alone the Black Sea, but Petersburg was founded in 1704 to replace both Archangel, Russia's principal port and trading centre, and Moscow, the ancient capital. A new and portentous landmark on the Baltic horizon, St Petersburg, closer to Amsterdam and London than Archangel, developed rapidly under the direction of its founder as a commercial port, as a naval base and, finally, a capital city. After 1714 St Petersburg was the place from which Russia was governed by the Tsar, the senate and, in due course, by the central offices of state. It was here, too, that foreign envoys most frequently arrived and took their leave. A review of the ceremonial observed on one such occasion, set against the background of the etiquette followed in similar circumstances in the previous age, may tell us something about the difference between the ethos of the late Muscovite and that of the early Imperial period.

In the reign of Alexis Mikhailovich every ceremonial act had its meaning. The degree of respect felt in the Kremlin for a particular visitor could be measured by the number of points at which he would be met by carefully chosen representatives of the Tsar. The scene in the porch of the palace was a dazzling display of wealth and authority. The courtiers and men of service lining the steps and gangway carpeted with oriental rugs and hung with sumptuous fabrics, wore garments of velvet, watered silk and lamé, lent for the occasion by the palace wardrobe, and carried halberds and partisans. An audience of the Tsar was planned to the very last detail, its slow and stately pace helped to create an atmosphere of timelessness. At the final and semi-private audience of Mayerberg, the ambassador of the Emperor Leopold I, held in April 1662, the Tsar was dressed 'simply' in a kaftan of flowered silk brocade trimmed with sable and fastened by clasps decorated with precious stones. He wore a pectoral cross and carried an ivory staff set with diamonds. His head-dress was a tall fur cap decorated with pearls and precious stones. Guarding his throne were four sons of the most prominent boyars armed with ceremonial axes studded with jewels and wearing cloth-of-silver tunics. The envoy and his suite were introduced by a secretary of the *duma* and it was through him that the Tsar enquired after their health. On receiving a reassuring answer, he bared his head and drank the health of the Emperor from a crystal goblet filled with mead. The envoys responded by drinking from silver-gilt cups filled with wine.

The Tsar spoke directly to the envoys only to send a brief message of compliments to the Emperor.

By 1720 everything had changed, not only the century but also the place and, above all, the style of diplomatic proceedings which was now brisk, businesslike and devoid of symbolism. Everyone seems to be in a hurry. The final audience of the Polish envoy is arranged at short notice for a Sunday because the Tsar has to leave St Petersburg in a matter of hours. Formality is reduced to a minimum: a few days earlier the Tsar himself had called on the envoy. Everyone is on the move, and no longer on land but by water, the coach and six has been replaced by the pinnace, one might just as well be in Venice or Amsterdam. The envoy and his suite are brought to the building occupied by the senate in five launches, the one carrying the ambassador is upholstered in green velvet and trimmed with gold braid. The ceremonial is half naval, half military. Out of the five officials and dignitaries deputed to receive and escort the envoys, three are army officers, the two civilians are the president and vice-president of the Board of Justice, a high-born Russian and a Baltic German. To greet the delegation flags are hoisted on a nearby galley. The soldiers in the company of guards drawn up at the entrance dip their colours and present arms to the roll of drums. The Tsar – it is a fair guess that he is wearing the uniform of a colonel of the Preobrazhenskii guards regiment – receives the ambassador standing at the foot of his throne and addresses him directly in a short speech. One by one, the envoys kiss the Tsar's hand but Peter, unlike his father, does not need to use a basin, a jug of water and a napkin to purify the spot that has been defiled by the lips of heretics. As the Poles depart, the flags are lowered and the guns in the fortress of SS Peter and Paul fire a thunderous salute. The ambassador did not record his reflections on this episode, but he would have been a poor observer indeed if he had failed to notice that he had visited a new world.

The exigencies of war made Peter a military leader and caused him to value discipline, organization and regularity in all things. The experience of military life and of the battlefield put him into contact with men of all stations, brought home to him the value of courage, initiative and competence and taught him to judge individuals by their merit rather than by the traditional standards of high birth and fortune. Long before the concept of meritocracy was formulated, Peter came to hold the view that promotion to any kind of rank or office must depend on the fitness of the aspirant to perform his duty. Carried to its logical conclusion, the principle might have put an end to hereditary monarchy in Russia. The conflict between the Tsar and the Tsarevich Alexis (who died in prison in 1718) and even more so the ordinance on the succession to the throne of 1724 were to show that Peter regarded neither primogeniture nor even kinship as decisive qualifications for the inheritance of the throne: the

Tsar reserved the right to appoint his own successor. Peter's moral position was a strong one. He saw his own life as one of service to his country and his people. From an early age he applied to himself with the utmost rigour the criterion of professional training and competence, climbing the ladder of promotion in the army from the grade of bombardier to that of lieutenant-colonel and rising on a parallel scale in the navy to the rank of rear-admiral. Outstanding merit was to be marked by the award of special honours. The Order of St Andrew the Apostle was instituted in 1698, that of St Catherine in 1714, on the birthday of the Tsarina, to commemorate the safe conclusion of the peace with the Turks in 1711.

Catherine, Peter's consort from 1712, formerly his concubine, to be crowned Empress in 1724, had saved Peter and Russia from disaster in the battle with the Turks on the River Pruth by keeping a cool head and prevailing on the enemy to enter into negotiation. The veracity of the attractive story according to which Catherine used her jewels and those of some other members of Peter's entourage to persuade the Grand Vizier to make peace with the encircled Russians on relatively lenient terms has yet to be proved. The preamble to the statute of the Order of St Catherine describes the desperate straits of the Russian forces and attributes their deliverance to divine intervention, but makes no reference to the decisive part played in the episode by Catherine herself. The order was to be known as the order of deliverance and to be dedicated to the Tsarina's patron saint. The tribute paid to the foundress and her sex is indirect: all the members of the order were to be women. Prayer was to be their principal business; the two practical concerns placed upon them were the redemption of slaves from barbaric captivity and the conversion of infidels to the Orthodox faith. The Tsar's true purpose in founding the order was to enhance the dignity of the Tsarina and to surround her with suitable companions. A slight improvement in the status of women at the highest level of Russian society followed as a natural consequence, but the predominantly religious character of the order shows that parity of esteem in the secular sphere was still unthinkable. The decision to establish an order in honour of St Alexander Nevsky was made in Peter's lifetime, but put into effect only after his death.

As to Catherine herself, it would appear that she possessed many of the qualities that Peter prized and his first wife, Eudoxia, though by no means wanting in ardour or physical grace, had lacked: vivacity, warmth, native intelligence and perhaps the ability to please by the simplicity and spontaneity of her demeanour. Her family origins were obscure, her domestic background was that of a Lutheran parsonage inclined towards Pietism, a good start for a *Hausfrau* destined to minister to the needs and eventually to share the labours of the royal shipwright.

ПРИКАЗАЛА ТОПИТЬ БАНЮ ХОЗАИНЪ СИДА НЕСК
ОЛКО ЧАСОВЪ ПРИНУЖДЕНЪ УЖЕ БЫЛЪ ЗАКРИЧАТЬ
СОБСТВЕНЫМЪ СВОИМЪ АЗЫКОМЪ АСЕСТРА ПРЕ
ДЛАГАЛА ЕМУ ПОЕГО ПРЕЖНЕМУ НАНЕМЕЦКОМЪ
АЗЫКЕ ПРИКАЗАНИЮ ЧТОБЪ ИЗВОЛИЛЪ ІПЇИТЬ
ВЪ БАНЮ ИРАБОТНИКЪ ПОВЕЛЪ ЕГО ХОЗАИНЪ ЛИШ
ТОЛКО ВСТУПИЛЪ КАДВЕРИ ТО ИЗАКРИЧАЛЪ ВИТЬ
А ТЕБЕ СКАЗАЛЪ ЧТО СІИ СЛОВА ОЗНАЧАЮТЪ ДАБЫ
НАКРЫВАТЬ НАСТОЛЪ АХЪ СУДАРЬ Ѿ ВЕЧАЛЪ РАБО
ТНИКЪ ЕСТЛИБЪ ВЫ ТАКЪ МНЕ ПРИКАЗАЛИ ТО
ВЫ КОНЕЧНО ИСПОЛНИЛЪ ВАШЕ ПОВЕЛЕНИЕ АТО И
САМИ ИЗВОЛИТЕ ЗНАТЬ ЧТО А ПОНЕМЕЦКИ
ГОВОВОРИТЬ НЕУМЕЮ СЕИ РУСКОИ СКАСКИ КОНЕЦЪ

Peter sponsored publication of children's books as part of his programme of education and enlightenment.

In private Peter and Catherine cultivated the life-style of a professional military or naval officer and his wife naturalized in Russia, with preference for all things Dutch in furniture and pictures. At masquerades Peter's favourite costume was that of a Dutch sailor, with Catherine correspondingly attired. Unlike his pious father, Peter had neither the time nor the inclination to attend endless church services, but on special occasions he would join for Holy Liturgy the choir of cantors (still designated as 'the patriarch's') who often accompanied him on his travels. Whitworth (the British ambassador), writing about the period before 1710, noted that the Tsar did not observe the fasts prescribed by the Church. From the point of view of any devout believer, this was a serious omission, fit to be likened to the brutish ways of the Lutheran heretics. It was only in 1716 that Peter obtained from the Patriarch of Constantinople a formal dispensation from fasting while on campaign for himself and for his army.

There is something engagingly modern and Anglo-Saxon about Peter's love of sailing and of dogs. The dogs (several of them, including Prints and Sobaka) appear to have been his constant companions. They went with him on the Caspian campaign and, when the weather turned cold in December, were provided with warm bedding and sheepskin coats.

Towards the end of his reign, the Tsar tried to introduce his subjects to the convivial informality of the social gatherings which he must have attended at the houses of the many foreigners in his service and also during his visits to the Netherlands in 1697 and 1716–17. John Perry, the English engineer who spent many years in Petrine Russia, notes that previously it had been the custom in Russia at all entertainments for women not to be admitted into the presence of men, except sometimes to offer visitors a dram of brandy before returning to their own apartments. At some point before Perry's return to England in 1712, the Tsar had already made it known that he wanted women to be invited to weddings and other public entertainments and to be received in the same room, and that the evenings should end in music and dancing. In 1718, in a deliberate effort to break down the barriers between the sexes, the social groups and the nationalities in St Petersburg, Peter decreed that assemblies were to be held. 'Assambleiia,' the Tsar explained,

> is a French term, the meaning of which cannot be rendered in Russian in a single word: it means free time, a gathering in a private house not only for entertainment but also for business, an opportunity for people to meet one another and talk about their concerns and be entertained at the same time. The way in which to arrange assemblies is set out below point by point, pending such time as they become a custom.

The hosts, the ordinance continues, should announce that all may come to their house, men and women alike. The parties should begin between four and five o'clock and end not later than ten. The guests may arrive and leave at any time they choose between these hours. The host should neither meet nor escort his guests, or offer them any food or drink and need not even be at home, but should just clear a few rooms and provide tables, candles, drink and some games. The guests should be free to sit, stand, walk about or play games without ceremony, under pain of draining a large goblet of spirits and should only bow to one another as they arrive and leave. The following ranks are to attend: officers and *dvoriane*, also prominent merchants and leading craftsmen, as well as higher government servants. The same applies to the female sex, to the wives and daughters of the above. Livery servants and footmen are not to attend, but should wait in the ante-chamber. Tsar Peter often appeared at the assemblies and took the opportunity to exercise his grim sense of humour, ordering the most aged of the men present to lead off the first dance, truly a *danse macabre*, a humiliating homage paid by the old age to the new.

A family man only in his few spare moments, Peter nevertheless gave some thought to marriage as an institution. Perry relates that, in order to put an end to 'blind bargain' marriages, the Tsar made it a rule that no young couple should be married without their own free liking and consent and should see something of one another during the six weeks before the wedding. It is obvious that Perry had in mind the ordinance of 1702 which also abolished the penalty for the non-fulfilment of contracts of engagement concluded between the families of the parties concerned. What Perry does not say is that the ordinance in question encroached on the area of ecclesiastical jurisdiction, whose exercise was in any event hampered by the vacancy in the patriarchate. In 1721 the ecclesiastical interregnum came to an end with the appointment of a governing Synod; in 1722 the Tsar issued a further ordinance forbidding parents and masters to force their children and serfs into marriage. It appears that in many cases the future spouses, whether from shame or fear, still did not dare to protest against being overborne. The objections, the ordinance continues, are made only after the event when disagreements arise between the parties. In order to prevent this from happening, the parents of both bride and bridegroom are required to swear that their children are not being married under duress. Although the ordinance made no formal distinction between the children of freemen and serfs, it required parents who were *dvoriane* or townspeople to swear an oath, whereas in respect of their subordinates they had only to make a declaration in writing.

In 1723 the length of the marriage service was shortened, possibly in deference to the Tsar's impatience with the intrusion of religion into everyday life. The minimum age for marriage had been fixed at twenty for men and seventeen for women within the law on the mode of inheritance of 1714. It is not clear whether this restriction was observed by the ecclesiastical authorities. Extra-marital sexual relations did not shock the Tsar; his indulgent attitude was prompted by populationist as much as by humanitarian considerations. Noting that the Emperor Charles V had punished fornication by death, Peter remarked that Russia could not afford such losses.

'What cannot active government perform, new-moulding man?'
asked James Thomson nodding in the direction of 'immortal Peter'.
As befits the social engineer, Peter was also an organizer of culture.
In the midst of his other preoccupations he did much not only to
promote learning by virtually founding the Academy of Sciences,
but also to inculcate in his subjects a mentality similar to his own,
secular and forward-looking. By the use of visual aids such as fire-
work displays, triumphal processions, transparencies and medals, he
introduced their beholders to the symbolic imagery of the modern
age. For the diffusion of ideas and the transmission of information,
he resorted, as any propagandist would, to the printing press, to the
publication of books and of a periodical – the first Russian newspaper,
Vedomosti, began to appear in 1703. It was renamed *Sankt Peterburgskie
Vedomosti* in 1728 after Peter's death and continued up to 1917. But
the Slavonic typeface in use during the early years of his reign,
being awkward to make and none too easy to read, was ill fitted for
the production and reception of print.

*Peter the Great is received at the Court of France by Louis XV (then
still a child), drawing by Desmarets, 1717.*

The necessary change was made on the initiative and with the active participation of Tsar Peter in the years 1707 and 1708. The new secular lettering, which replaced the hieratic print in non-ecclesiastical publications, was clear, bold and distinctly Latin in appearance, well suited to the needs of the growing numbers of those whom the demands of military or government service compelled to read or, in the case of foreigners, to read Russian. It would be hard to find a more telling and more pleasing symbol of the new age than the *grazhdanskii shrift*. Characteristically, the first work to be printed in the new type was a manual of geometry published in 1708.

As indigenous production was slow to get under way, many of the books published in Peter's reign were translations from western European languages. A propagandist more concerned with official supply than with public demand, the Tsar considered the need for translations, and therefore also of translators, to be unlimited, especially in applied science: mathematics, mechanics, surgery, botany, military and civil architecture, hydraulics and the like.

Peter's interest, aroused during his first visit to western Europe, in all matters relating to aids to learning and scientific research – books, specimens, instruments – and his wish to acquire them, grew stronger with the years and eventually extended to the recruitment of scientists. This may be seen from the detailed instructions which the Tsar gave his librarian, J.D. Schumacher, for his expedition to Western Europe in 1721–2. Among other things, Schumacher was to make drawings from models available in observatories, to find out about the acoustic tube from Father Sebastian (Truchet), to ask Monsieur du Verney about anatomical specimens made from wax, to invite Duvernoy, the anatomist of Paris, and Monsieur Delisle, the geographer and cartographer, to enter the service of His Majesty, to invite Professor (Johann Christian) Wolff, to discuss with Orfireus (or Orffyré) his invention of the *perpetuum mobile*, to order portable and naval thermometers from Fahrenheit and machines and instruments appertaining to experimental physics from Musschenbroek, to engage in England a man who knew how to conduct scientific experiments and to make the necessary instruments, to visit private and public museums and collections, and to try to plan a complete library for His Imperial Majesty. Schumacher was nothing if not *akkuratnyi* in his investigations and was able to report to His Majesty *inter alia* that, 'The University Library at Oxford almost equals that at Cambridge, the former being richer in manuscripts, the latter, since the acquisition of the library of the bishop of Ely, in printed books.'

Peter was not a systematic student of any subject: he satisfied his very considerable curiosity by questioning directly such people as Bruce, the master of the ordnance, Dr Robert Erskine, his personal physician, or possibly Henry Farquharson, the mathematician, and no doubt many others both in and outside Russia. Peter appears to have developed a liking for books in early manhood. The story goes that in 1694 he reprimanded the Patriarch for the neglected and disorderly state of his library and that four years later he expressed amazement at the size of the library of the Archbishop of Canterbury (at Lambeth Palace): he had never before seen so many books in one place. He was a desultory reader: his taste ranged from Caesar (probably read to him in translation) to the tale of Peter and Fevroniia, the manuscript of which apparently he took with him on the Caspian campaign. It tells of the passionate love of a prince for a simple peasant girl. He renounces his throne for her and even death cannot part them. Did Peter see some connection here between Fevroniia and his consort, Catherine?

The Russian and Slavonic books and manuscripts owned by the Tsar and members of the ruling family in the seventeenth century had been for the most part of a religious character: the Scriptures, works of biblical exegesis, writings of the Fathers of the Church, lives of the saints, homilies, liturgies and theological treatises. Only in the second half of the century were these collections augmented by items of a secular nature, including some in languages other than Russian, whose subjects have been described as geography, medicine, the teaching of foreign languages and, oddly enough, equitation. These books and manuscripts, which give the impression of having been accumulated at random before being forgotten in an attic and, except for schoolbooks, more often acquired by gift than by purchase, formed the inherited part of the Tsar's library. Some of the items added to it during his reign to make a total of about 1,600 printed books conform to the standards of traditional Muscovite piety, whereas others could be thought to offend it by showing an unhealthy curiosity in Roman Catholicism and Protestantism. The majority bear witness to Peter's intense interest in the intellectual achievements and practical knowledge of that dynamic new world which he wished his country to enter.

The subjects best represented after religious literature are: navigation and shipbuilding, military science (including artillery and fortification), history and heraldry, geography (including cosmography and atlases), architecture (including landscape architecture and garden design), *belles lettres*, science (mathematics, physics, chemistry) and technology. Two items are also connected with the person of Bruce: Newton's *Philosophiae Naturalis Principia Mathematica*, one of the two copies originally owned by Bruce, and the *Kosmotheoros* by Constantine Huygens, which was published in Bruce's Russian translation in 1717. The presence in the collection of only two treatises on economics, one a German work entitled *The Prince's Statecraft or the inexhaustible golden well by the use of which the ruler may make himself strong and enrich his subjects* (1703), the other the French version of John Law's *Money and Trade Considered*, suggests that Peter had little interest or faith in economic doctrine. However, at some point he must have thought well enough of the German work to have singled it out for translation into Russian. The same indifference lends credence to the assertion that Peter, whose interest in foreign trade was widely known, never grasped its mechanics.

Even more closely connected with Peter's attraction to the spirit and method of scientific enquiry was his interest in the curiosities of nature and in scientific instruments. In these areas too he was a buyer and a collector. In 1717 he bought in Holland for 15,000 gulden a collection of 'land and sea animals', birds, snakes and insects from the naturalist Albertus Seba; for 30,000 gulden the cabinet of anatomical specimens prepared by the famous Dr Frederik Ruysch over a period of fifty years; and a collection of scientific instruments from Pieter van Musschenbroek. A description of Seba's collection enumerates seventy-two chests of shells from the East and West Indies, 400 jars containing strange and monstrous animals preserved in vinegar, and a further 400 jars containing, among other items, 'toads turning into fish' (or rather vice versa: axolotls) and specimens of American frogs 'whose offspring breed from the spine' (the Surinam toad). Also 'a Virginian toad with horns and long ears' (a horned toad), crocodiles, armadillos, caymans, salamanders, baboons, flying snakes, flying fish, octopuses, sea cats, sea mice, tarantulas and other spiders, etc., and thirty-two chests containing butterflies. Further, Asian, African and American reptiles, mineral specimens from the East Indies, China, Hungary and the whole of Germany, stuffed birds and many more heterogeneous objects including artefacts from Asia and Africa.

Ruysch's and Seba's collections were shortly transferred to the *Kunstkammer* or palace of rarities, the first Russian museum, opened in 1714. In 1718, realizing the potential scientific value of native archaeological finds, Tsar Peter ordered his subjects to inform the authorities of the whereabouts of monsters, antiquities, inscriptions and curiosities, and offered the following rewards: for human monsters handed in dead – 10 roubles; the same, animal – 5 roubles; birds – 3 roubles; for live human monsters – 100 roubles; the same, animal – 15 roubles; live birds – 7 roubles. If the object was particularly strange that reward would be increased, if the opposite it would be reduced. Dead specimens should be preserved in vinegar or vodka and tightly closed to prevent deterioration. The Tsar's pharmacy would reimburse the cost of the alcohol. The great monarch had an uncommon eye for detail.

The Tsar also owned a globe so vast that it had to be housed in a special shed in the care of a keeper who at one time had indented for four pounds of machine oil to lubricate the bearings of his exhibit, thirty arshins of linen to keep its surface clean and half a pood of tallow candles. The object, the famous Gottorp Globe, built about

The wedding feast of Peter and Catherine, his second wife, in February 1712.

1650 and presented by King Frederick IV of Denmark to Tsar Peter in 1713, was in fact a planetarium. The spectators entered by a small opening in the lower section and sat on a circular bench. The globe was rotated on its axis by a drive which should have been connected to a water wheel, but was probably cranked by hand. The planets painted on the inner surface and illuminated by candles rose and set in relation to an artificial horizon. On the surface of the globe was painted a map of the world.

The inscription on one of the medals struck in Peter's honour proclaimed on his behalf: 'I am a student and seek teachers.' This exhibition of modesty and inadequacy was bound to command respect, but Peter was a shrewd enough politician to realize that to stand on the threshold of the modern world in an attitude of admiration was of little practical benefit, whereas much prestige could be gained from establishing direct relations with scientists and scholars. He both deserved and needed to be known as the monarch who:

Sredí voénnykh bur'
Naúki nam otkrýl'

'Amid the storms of war he led us towards learning.' But the demands made on his time by politics and war and sheer lack of funds did not allow him to become a patron of scholars and philosophers on any significant scale. Leibniz, who insinuated himself into Peter's favour (rather than was head-hunted by him), received his pension as secret councillor only once. Baron Huyssen, Peter's chief propagandist for western Europe, was required by the terms of his contract (made in 1702) among other things to persuade Dutch, German and other scholars to dedicate to the Tsar and members of his family or to his ministers works relating to history, politics and mechanics and to write articles in praise of Russia. Some articles were written, mostly by Huyssen himself, the rest did not come about.

There is much more to the mind and personality of Peter the Great than the aspects that have just been examined. To have created the impression of some high-minded pedant, some kind of Prince Consort of an heroic Catherine, would have been misleading. Peter was, as we all know, a man of action, an epic figure tainted by many vices and richly endowed with virtues and talents. One of these gifts was an intellectual curiosity so intense and so wide-ranging that it enabled its owner to seize a fundamental truth, to intuit the wholeness of modern culture. It was David Hume who said that, 'We cannot reasonably expect that a piece of woollen cloth will be brought to perfection in a nation which is ignorant of astronomy, or where ethics is neglected.' Now Peter did instruct Farquharson to teach and popularize astronomy and some cloth was manufactured in Russia. What Hume meant is that material and intellectual culture are interdependent, that any process of modernization is at once technical and intellectual. This realization determined the modernity of Peter's *mentalité* or idiosyncrasy, but his actions did not extend it to his country and his people as a whole. His social and financial policies, often dictated by the force of circumstances, did not release from among the masses the ambition, the initiative or the enterprise without which capitalism could not be generated and the entry into the modern world effected.

CHAPTER IX

Klyuchevsky and the Course of Russian History

PAUL DUKES

Portraits of V.O. Klyuchevsky show a modest, bearded, bespectacled, slightly dishevelled figure who would not have looked out of place at the beginning of the century in the library of the British Museum. They do not fit in at all with Kipling's assertion that the Russians were fine fellows until they tucked in their shirts and began to ape the more cultivated citizens of other European empires. But how could such an evident gentleman achieve a sympathetic understanding of a national history that was widely deemed in the West to contain little that was creditable or even civilized? It was Klyuchevsky's achievement to present an account of Russian development that was not only coherent but also persuasive, at least until it neared the public events of his own lifetime. Then, as we shall see, he came up against some insuperable problems.

Vasily Osipovich Klyuchevsky was born in a small village 200 miles or so to the south-east of Moscow on 16 January 1841. His father was a parish priest. It was customary for Orthodox white clergy (as opposed to the black, monastic clergy) to marry and live among the people. So, from an early age, Vasily became acquainted not only with the Church Slavonic of Holy Writ but also with the local language of the peasants. Already, therefore, he was in the early stages of the formation of a distinctive literary style. In 1850, his father was accidentally drowned while returning home from a shopping expedition for cucumbers at the local market. Vasily's consequent shock has been deemed responsible for a persistent stammer. However, this did not prevent the young man from developing later a talent for oratory at least as outstanding as that for writing. Indeed, his most impressive and largest work, *The Course of Russian History*, was to begin its existence as a series of lectures.

At his father's death, his mother took Vasily and his two sisters to the nearby town of Penza, where he went to the church school. He seemed destined to follow his ancestral line, and entered the local theological seminary at the age of fifteen in 1856, the year after the accession of Tsar Alexander II. The fiasco of the Crimean War had just come to an end, only to be followed by mass popular unrest, and

V.O. Klyuchevsky, a historical pioneer of the longue durée, *who found his own liberal vision of a European Russia clouded by the contradictions and pessimism of his own times.*

the widespread apprehension that this would become uncontrollable if some drastic steps were not taken. Against such a background, possibly because of it, Klyuchevsky became so interested in history that he decided to give up the church and devote himself instead to the study of the past. Overcoming many difficulties by 1861, he managed to enrol in the University of Moscow. There, his professor was S.M. Solovyov, a respected if unexciting speaker and a voluminous if 'scissors-and-paste' writer. In 1879, still young for an academic, but already experienced as a teacher and writer, Klyuchevsky became the ailing Solovyov's successor. Before his own retirement and death in 1911, he established such a reputation as a lecturer that no colleague could schedule classes at the same hour as Klyuchevsky's. His lectures were so popular that they had to be put into print by public demand.

What was the secret of Klyuchevsky's success? Undoubtedly, he was an outstanding scholar, who had shown technical mastery in such early works as *Lives of the Early Russian Saints as a Source of History* (1871) and *Accounts of Foreigners concerning the Muscovite State* (1866). But it is possible to make expert use of documents without the ability to keep even a few devotees awake, let alone fill a hall to overflowing. More pertinent therefore in this respect was Klyuchevsky's considerable acting ability, the combination of the historical with the histrionic. Among those who sat at his feet was the great singer, Chaliapin, who recalled as part of his

109

preparation for the challenging role of Boris Godunov an extended interview with Klyuchevsky, who provided a most lively account of the life and times of Tsar Boris. The opera, it will be recalled, was taken by Mussorgsky from the verse drama by Pushkin, who in turn made use of the *History of the Russian State* by N.M. Karamzin. Chaliapin's consultation with Klyuchevsky was to result no doubt in some reinjection of the real Boris into his inimitable portrayal of that unfortunate Tsar. Are there some echoes of Klyuchevsky's evocation of early seventeenth-century Russia in Chaliapin's early twentieth-century recordings?

But Klyuchevsky's great popularity was not simply a consequence of his ability to draw convincing word portraits of Boris Godunov, Ivan the Terrible, Peter the Great and other outstanding individuals. He was also able to incorporate his purple passages into an overall structure that was as well-shaped as it was colourful. He gave his *Course* a clear sense of direction, beginning with a statement of aims. He wanted to present not just the simple story of the past of the motherland, but rather an account of the many-sided activities of her peoples. In other words, he wished to create 'an historical sociology'. Such an aim could be fully achieved only if national history was seen as a part of a larger process, in which outside as well as internal pressures were given their due weighting. Only thus, for example, could it be understood why the Germans, as peaceful and friendly as any people in Europe at the beginning of the nineteenth century, had been transformed into aggressors who had advanced power as a principle of international relations and forced all the peoples of continental Europe to be under arms. Looking at Russian history in such a comparative manner, Klyuchevsky believed understanding of it would be increased by looking at the basic conditions of Russian development along with those of west European counterparts.

The fundamental fact of Russian history was colonization in a boundless plain, continually working itself out through successive phases. First, there was Kievan Rus on the River Dnieper, urban and commercial. Next, after domestic dissension and the Mongol invasion, came Rus on the Upper Volga, with separate principalities and free agriculture. There ensued expansion down the Volga and the Don to create Great Rus, Muscovy, with tsars and boyars, and regimented agriculture. From the beginning of the seventeenth to the middle of the nineteenth century, settlement grew from the White and Baltic Seas to the Black and the Caspian, from Poland to Siberia. This was the All-Russian period, imperial and noble and serf. The basic scheme of his subject was expanded by the great man through eighty-six lectures bringing his account up to the period of his own early manhood in the 1860s, the decade of the Emancipation of the Serfs and other 'Great Reforms'. Klyuchevsky concluded by confessing that his own generation had failed to solve the subsequent dual problem of which ideas should be imported from west European civilization and how Russia could be prepared for their reception. But he was sure that posterity would succeed.

Publication of *The Course of Russian History* began in 1904, the year before the first Russian Revolution, and continued throughout the rest of a never less than turbulent decade. Klyuchevsky was preparing the fifth and final volume for publication in the months leading up to his death in the spring of 1911. And so the period

Chaliapin in the title role of Boris Godunov, in 1913. He drew on an interview with Klyuchevsky for his portrayal of the tsar.

of his own adulthood and its wider setting were very much on his mind at this sombre time. No doubt his grave illness was partly responsible for the pessimistic mood of his final writings about them, but his arguments remain telling. He observed that, the closer Russia had drawn together with western Europe, the more difficult it had become to establish the manifestations of popular freedom. This was because:

> . . . the means of west European culture, falling into the hands of some narrow strata of society, have been turned to their defence rather than the advantage of the country, strengthening social inequality, have been changed into a weapon for the many-sided exploitation of the culturally defenceless masses, lowering the level of their social consciousness and strengthening their class animosity, by which they are prepared for revolt rather than freedom.

He was critical of the Emperors Paul, Alexander I and Nicholas I, who 'possessed Russia rather than ruling it, introducing their own dynastic interest rather than that of the state, exercising their own will, not wanting and not knowing how to understand the needs of the people'. He implied that the later Emperors, Alexander II, Alexander III and Nicholas II, were little if at all less self-centred. Meanwhile, the tragedy of the opposition was that 'the patriot enlightened at government expense was struggling against his own country, while not believing in the power of enlightenment or in the future of the motherland'. It was equally tragic that:

> The law of the life of backward states or peoples among those which have outstripped it is that the need for reform arises earlier than the people is ready for reform. The necessity for accelerated movement in pursuit leads to the over-hasty adoption of the ways of others.

Klyuchevsky's great work demonstrated the impossibility of writing a 'Whig' version of the history of his motherland. While not active politically, he certainly shared the aspirations of European liberalism in its broader sense. He sought to show that Russia was not so dissimilar from its fellow European states that it could not follow the path of their development. However belatedly, the tsarist government would move from unrestrained absolutism to some kind of constitutional moderation. But, if his British counterparts could present without difficulty the story of a stable parliamentary regime evolving after the Glorious and Bloodless Revolution of 1688 and surviving whatever buffets in the years leading up to 1914, Klyuchevsky found his own account falling apart from the 1860s onwards, perhaps even before. Furthermore, his overall conception produced other structural weaknesses. The concentration on the Great Russian story meant neglect of the stories of the other peoples of the Empire: Ukrainian, Baltic, Transcaucasian, and so on. There was an under-emphasis of the impact of the Mongol invasion.

The massacre of demonstrators in St Petersburg, January 1905: the start of the internal disturbances that darkened Klyuchevsky's view of Russian history in his final years.

Opposition movements, whether from an insurgent peasantry or a radical intelligentsia, went largely unmentioned. And there was a significant failure to give due weight to international relations, increasingly important as the grasp for world power by Germany, noticed by Klyuchevsky in his introductory chapters, became ever more insistent.

After the outbreak of the First World War and the Russian Revolutions of 1917, the historical sociology of a continental scholar who might have worked in the British Museum was replaced by that of two others of his like who actually did work there,

Marx and Lenin. But this does not mean that Klyuchevsky was forgotten, even in the Soviet Union, ·where many of his works have been reissued or published for the first time, and the whole corpus subjected to searching analysis. The most complete Soviet study, by M.V. Nechkina, asserts:

> He gave Russian scholarship one of the most brilliant conceptions of the historical past of the country – contradictory, incomplete, but full of problems. And when did he give it, at what time? Between the first Russian revolutionary situation and the eve of October, at a tense, stormy epoch. He forced thousands of minds to think about a multiplicity of questions, many of which he himself could not answer. He enriched with these questions both those who agreed with him and those who did not. Moreover, he drew on the basis of his own scheme such lively, artistic pictures and portraits of the people of past centuries that are impossible to forget. For some he has developed an interest in the history of Russia, for others he has aroused it for the first time.

Even western scholars who do not share Nechkina's world view would accept much of her appraisal. All of us would join together to lament the fact that so little of *The Course of Russian History* has been translated competently into English. The version done by C.J. Hogarth is scarcely better than none at all. Too careful to be imaginative, but insufficiently skilled to be accurate, Hogarth produced a travesty that is often opaque and sometimes nonsensical. Fortunately, some of the chapters on Peter the Great, and others on the rise of

A fatal turning point? The assassination of Alexander II, emancipator of the serfs.

his predecessor Romanovs have been rendered into English in an acceptable manner. But the grand sweep of the work as a whole remains inaccessible to all those who cannot read Russian.

A continental colleague recently described an attempt to write a study of Tsar Ivan the Terrible. He began by consulting as many previous works on Ivan as he could find, leaving till last one which he thought would be well out of date and of little use in any way, but which he soon began to consider so pertinent and perspicacious that he could no longer continue his own project. And where had he found his inimitable model? In the second volume of *The Course of Russian History*, by Vasily Osipovich Klyuchevsky.

CHAPTER X

Hrushevsky and the Ukraine's 'Lost' History

THOMAS PRYMAK

Michael Hrushevsky (1866–1934) is one of the most important Ukrainian figures of the modern era. Both for his admirers and for his detractors he was a legend in his own time. In the eyes of his supporters, this bearded and bespectacled professor was by far the greatest of modern Ukrainian historians, the author of a monumental ten-volume *History of Ukraine-Rus* which documented the history of the Ukrainian people from Kievan Rus to the dawn of the modern era. Hrushevsky was also known as the principal organizer of modern Ukrainian scholarship, the most celebrated spokesman for the decentralization and federalization of pre-revolutionary Russia, the first president of the short-lived but precedent-setting Ukrainian People's Republic of 1917–18, and one of the most influential historians living in the Soviet Union during the 1920s. In fact, as early as the revolutionary years of 1917–18 his compatriots had already admiringly dubbed him the 'father' of his country.

Of course Hrushevsky's critics interpreted these activities in their own special way. In the eyes of the supporters of Tsar Nicholas II, for example, Hrushevsky was the 'arch-traitor', an Austrian, Polish or German agent who had invented an 'artificial' Ukrainian language and dreamed up a false scheme of Russian and Ukrainian history. Before the Revolution of 1917, Russian monarchists saw 'the magical hand of Hrushevsky' behind almost every manifestation of the forbidden Ukrainian national movement. Later on, the defeated 'Whites' of the 1920s, especially émigré Russian liberals, tended to see Hrushevsky as the radical Ukrainian separatist who, in 1917, had helped the 'Reds' to disrupt the provisional government and cause the downfall of Russia. By the 1930s, moreover, Soviet authors too discounted him as a 'bourgeois Ukrainian nationalist' who was plotting against the Soviet state. Under Stalin, Khrushchev and Brezhnev his name could not be mentioned in print without an accompanying series of opprobrious adjectives and he was always labelled 'an uncompromising enemy of the Russian and Ukrainian peoples'.

What was so special about Hrushevsky's historical and political ideas and why did they arouse such strong objections on the part

*Michael Hrushevsky in his Lemberg (Lvov) study sometime
before 1914.*

of his various critics? The answer, of course, lies in Hrushevsky's
basic approach to history and the way it affected his scholarship and
his public life.

Michael Hrushevsky was brought up in the strict tradition of
Ukrainian radical populism which originated at the time of the poet
Taras Shevchenko (1814–61), whose fiery and melancholic verses had
elevated the language of the Ukrainian countryfolk to the level of a
profound and flexible literary medium. Shevchenko had also rejected
the old term 'Little Russia' and used the name 'Ukraine' in a revolutionary way that stressed national and social rather than geographical
and regional themes. His followers, Hrushevsky included, did not
think of themselves as the quaint southern branch of the Russian
national tree, but rather simply as Ukrainians who had national
characteristics of their own which had always differed from those
of the people of Muscovy or Novgorod. With Shevchenko, the
Ukrainian national awakening was born.

It was Hrushevsky's lifelong goal to complete this awakening by
documenting the history of his people from their earliest origins to
contemporary times. Other historians had made a start by talking

about the 'two Russian nationalities' and pointing out the 'federal' character of the ancient state of Kiev Rus; Hrushevsky only went one step further by claiming Kievan Rus as primarily the heritage of the modern Ukrainian people and postulating that imperial Russia had its origins in fourteenth-century Muscovy rather than eleventh-century Kiev. He thus rejected the old Muscovite dynastic theory of the transfer of the state, the *translatio imperii* from the Kievan south to the Muscovite north and he directed the 'Great Russians', as they were then called, to look to their own lakes and forests for the pre-historic origins of the modern Russian people while leaving Kiev and the Ukrainian steppes for the modern Ukrainians. After publishing several volumes of his great *History of Ukraine-Rus*, Hrushevsky summarized his position with this caution:

> Certainly, there was no Ukrainian nation *in its final form* in the ninth and tenth centuries, and so in the twelfth to the fourteenth centuries there was neither a Great Russian nor a Ukrainian nation in the form of our contemporary understanding. However, I, like any other historian who sees his duty in the investigation of national evolution, am expected to begin with the early origin of the formation of a nation. For this reason, the cultural, economic, and political life of the southern group of East Slavic tribes from which finally emerged the Ukrainian nation, should be a part of the history of Ukraine – and certainly with greater justification than the inclusion of the 'Kievan period' into the history of the Great Russian state, a scheme otherwise known as 'Russian history'.

Thus, while acknowledging that the term 'Ukraine' might be a relatively new one, Hrushevsky was still able to trace the history of his people and land through many political ascendencies and eras – Kievan, Lithuanian, Polish and imperial Russian – to modern times.

In his great narrative, Hrushevsky painted the Kievan era in bright colours and saw the assimilation of the principalities of western and southern Rus into the medieval Lithuanian state as a peaceful process which naturally followed the shattering impact of the Mongol invasion. However, when Lithuania united with the Kingdom of Poland to form the Polish-Lithuanian Commonwealth, Hrushevsky painted the situation of the Ukrainians in darker colours and saw the defence of Orthodoxy against Polish attempts to spread Roman Catholicism or church union among the Ukrainians in terms of a national cultural struggle. This conflict climaxed in the great Cossack revolt of 1648, which championed Orthodoxy and the rights of the common people against the aristocratic Catholic Commonwealth. Military alliance and political association with Orthodox Muscovy followed and Ukraine was slowly absorbed into what became known in the time of Peter the Great as the Russian Empire. This process of assimilation was never complete, however, and in the nineteenth century the poet Shevchenko and a circle of other progressive figures inspired a national rebirth which recalled the romantic glories of the Cossack era. It must be stressed, however, that throughout this narrative Hrushevsky always concentrated upon the experience and struggles of the common people and only described the transient state structures as they impinged upon the life of the common folk. In this way, Hrushevsky was able to see continuity and process through the various political ascendencies and eras and give unity and a national significance to this process.

This was what came to be called his 'scheme' and during the first third of the twentieth century, especially during the revolutionary era and the 1920s when both Russian and Ukrainian historians were condemning imperialism, and when decentralization and the renaissance of the minority peoples of the USSR were prominent motifs, it came to be accepted, not only by virtually all Ukrainian historians, but also by most Belorussian and Lithuanian historians, as well as by some Poles. Hrushevsky's ideas also influenced some particularly innovative Russian historians who linked the history of the common people to the evolution of state structures. However, Stalin's 1930s purges brought these developments to an abrupt end.

*V*ladimir the Great (980–1015), the first unifier of the Slav states, who introduced Orthodox Christianity. His empire collapsed, in part due to complicated inheritance laws, and in part due to a lack of infrastructure.

*T*aras Grigorievich Shevchenko (1814–61), poet of the Ukraine
and social reformer who stood out against the policy of Russification,
stressing the past glories of an independent Ukraine.

In 1934, while on vacation in the Caucasus, Hrushevsky died under mysterious circumstances. He was given a state funeral and buried in Kiev, the capital of the Ukrainian SSR. But, within two weeks of his death, the Ukrainian Academy of Sciences could no longer publish materials about him and citation of his name as a reference became dangerous. The Communist Party press attacked him as a ringmaster of a vast anti-Soviet conspiracy, his politics were condemned as bourgeois, and his historical scheme was labelled as false. Members of his historical 'school' were publicly denounced and exiled to the gulag. Works by a new generation of historians more in tune with Stalin's policies of centralization and Russification once again claimed Kievan Rus primarily for Moscow and the Russian people.

But Hrushevsky's very real contribution to east European historiography could not be completely destroyed. After Hrushevsky's death, the critique of what he called 'the traditional scheme of Russian history' was further elaborated by Ukrainian scholars working in inter-war Poland and by Lithuanian scholars as well. After 1945, this tradition was carried on principally by Ukrainian, but also by Belorussian and Polish émigrés.

Once again, the principal point stressed by all these scholars was the existence of a Ukrainian historical process with its roots in Kievan Rus, a process distinct from that of Muscovy and imperial Russia, and a process which gave rise to the modern Ukrainian and, in part, Belorussian nations. As early as the turn of the century, the distinguished imperial Russian scholar, Vasili Klyuchevsky, had unconsciously recognized the legitimacy of this idea by emphasizing the distinction between commercial and internationally oriented Kievan Rus and agricultural and nationally isolated Muscovy, and by restricting his attention to the history of the 'Great Russian' people. As recently as the 1970s, Ukrainian Christians gave the same idea their conscious approval by launching the celebrations for 'the millennium of Christianity in Ukraine', a formula which is accepted both by the Orthodox and the Catholic wings of Ukrainian Christianity. Needless to say, 'the millennium of the Christening of Rus' is interpreted differently by the Soviet authorities and the legal Russian Orthodox Church who determined that most of the major public festivities would take place in Moscow and not in Kiev. The heart of the dispute, of course, remains the different conceptions of history elaborated by Hrushevsky, who first formulated a national scheme of history for the Ukrainian people, and by Russian, Soviet and a great many western scholars who continue to reject it.

The situation, however, remains fluid. In the West, discussion of Hrushevsky's ideas and of the legitimacy of the Ukrainian claim to the Kievan heritage has barely begun, while, in the USSR, a new political climate has brought Hrushevsky's histories out of the 're-stricted collections' (*spetsfondy*) and on to the public shelves of Soviet academic libraries. His name is now once again mentioned in print and it is recognized that the foremost contemporary Soviet authority on the origins of Rus, Boris Rybakov, quietly lifted some of his basic notions about Slavic antiquity from the works of Hrushevsky. The Ukrainian national intelligentsia has specifically asked for the rehabilitation of their foremost historian and a number of small but important steps have been taken in this direction. The publication of a multi-volume edition of Hrushevsky's *Collected Works* has been announced.

Kievan Rus 1054–1242.

All of these developments are indications of the continuing importance of Hrushevsky's historical ideas and the continuing political significance of his person. In the eyes of most Ukrainians, he remains the great scholar who completed the national awakening by giving them a national history quite distinct from that of the Russians, and then by translating this history into political terms by standing at the head of the revolutionary Ukrainian Republic of 1917–18. In the eyes of many Russians, Hrushevsky remains a controversial historian who threatens to deprive them of the 'mother of Russian cities', Kiev, and disrupt the unity of the Soviet state which they dominate. In the eyes of other Russians, Ukrainians and informed third parties, Hrushevsky and his historical scheme have become a test case by which promises of political reform, openness, and decentralization may be measured.

CHAPTER XI

Filling in the Blank Spots in Soviet History

YURI AFANASYEV

Yuri Afanasyev has become one of the leading popular advocates of the revaluation of domestic and world history in the Soviet Union. This includes dealing with controversial episodes in the Revolution's seventy-year history openly and objectively. Such views have plunged Afanasyev into the thick of controversy and polemic in the Soviet Union. Here he takes his argument further, in an interview with Albert Sirotkin of *Novosti*, given in 1988.

Question: *Is there any connection between perestroika in society and the rejuvenation of history as a science?*

There is a direct relationship between the two. The basic economic, social and cultural patterns in the USSR were shaped during the period of Stalinism. So were some very clichéd thoughts. We are now struggling to overcome the aftermath of this period. It is impossible to identify the heritage of a past which is hanging like a millstone around our necks, without looking back; without history.

For example, look at the period when we went over to a system of strict centralized planning. This was at the turn of the 1930s, when the words bore little resemblance to the deeds. Soviet society was losing its identity, we did not have a clear-cut idea of what we were as a social order – as a community of people. A spade had ceased to be called a spade!

Several generations of Soviet people have breathed a heavy ideological smog. History has been falsified. I believe the process was at its worst when the drive for perestroika began. Virtually every period, event and issue had been misrepresented until relatively recently. The majority of history books followed suit, with certain events being passed over in silence. Our own Soviet history suffered most, with almost everything that preceded perestroika being liable to a Stalinist interpretation.

At the turn of this century, French historians interpreted the history of France in such a way as to present some of the kings as republicans, while the rest were seen as anti-republicans. The

'Big Brother'? Josef Stalin at a 1935 celebration for the completion of the Moscow underground – one of the few legacies of the Stalinist era not under criticism and reappraisal in the Soviet Union today.

'republican' kings were the ones who extended the borders of the state, strengthened national unity and promoted the enrichment of France.

Stalin used to interpret Soviet history in much the same way, with the things he approved of being extolled by historians. Under Ivan the Terrible, who was fighting the boyars or nobles, positive achievements were viewed as the creation of punitive bodies, the *Oprichnina* (guards) and the police.

Before him, Ivan III began the unification of the Russian lands and produced the imperial ideology: Moscow, the Third Rome. Stalin liked Peter the Great for his barbaric methods of building a new Russia. It is for this reason that Soviet historians are now facing the difficult task of correcting the Stalinist vision of our history, beginning with the ancient Rus of 1,000 years ago.

Another aftermath of Stalinism is that the Soviet people have become used to a lop-sided view of our history and national heritage. Revolutionary democratic traditions were dished out without the inherent contradictions in them being explained – these were simply ignored.

Historical consciousness was maimed. And it is historical consciousness that forms our vision of labour; of the world; of our place in it; our ability to have a dialogue. Historical consciousness also determines the way in which the economy is run. Our fake national history inhibits the development of our economy today.

Take the aggressive attitude of some officials and many private citizens towards those who want to lease land or form a co-operative. Their attitude is dogmatic: black-and-white. It is their misfortune rather than their guilt, for this kind of mentality has been cultivated for decades in the intellectual world. All sorts of distortions and shortcuts in history have played their destructive part.

What do you think are the reasons?

There is one simple answer: Stalin's regime was unnatural, illegal and contradicted the ideas, traditions and history of socialism. It was imposed by force, using mass criminal reprisals. To make it appear legitimate there had to be a fake history. People had to think uniformly – to understand and believe things in the same, distorted way. We are now feeling the results. 'Sow the wind and reap the whirlwind,' as the saying goes.

Perestroika has shown clearly that the restoration of historical truth is a painful process and that passions will be running high. Let me remind the historians reading this of the notorious letter Nina Andreyeva wrote to *Sovetskaya Rossia* to justify Stalin's rule, and of the reply editorial article in *Pravda*. Or take the libel suit filed by a certain man against journalist Alex Adamovich for having allegedly humiliated Stalin in an article – a Moscow court dismissed the suit.

The treatment of our history and the restoration of historical truth have become two of the most acute and dramatic pages in the story of our society's process of renovation. My belief is that Stalinism is by no means a thing of the past.

Its system – comprising economic and hierarchic structures; privileges; management by injunction; as well as clichéd thinking – is being uncovered. All are beginning to see the 'blank spots' of history being filled in with colour, and this is creating some resistance to perestroika.

Over the seventy-one years of Soviet power, we have failed to attain the task as put to us by the founders of socialism: the alienation between the people and the means of economic production has not yet been overcome.

One cannot forecast the ways socialism will develop without a deep analysis of what has been done, of what we have achieved so far and of what we are yet to have – without a true history of socialism in the Soviet Union since 1917.

When we are told that what we have is real socialism, we begin to think the goal has been attained. This is designed to lull society and drag it back into the past. It is intended to preserve the remnants of the forged model of socialism as well as our fake history. This is another reason why historical truth is so urgent today.

Had we conducted in-depth theoretical and historical studies of these problems, we would perhaps have had a better idea of the alternative, unrealized directions for the development of Soviet society.

Why did the first attempt at perestroika and the democratization of society flop under Khrushchev after the 20th Party Congress in 1956? Why was it that the criticism of Stalin's personality cult was incomplete, while Stalinist structures survived and Stalinism itself existed in a modified form for another two decades, until it was again exposed at the April 1985 Plenum of the Communist Party's Central Committee?

We are thus facing the issue of alternatives, of the variability of history, and of the need to get rid of a dogmatized historical materialism which presents the path of Soviet society after the October Revolution as a straight course predetermined by certain 'laws'. We need to show the evolution of the ideas of socialism, of Lenin's views of the new society.

In the summer of 1917, on the eve of the October Revolution, the main tasks were to implement agrarian reform, socialize the means of production and create a Paris Commune-type authority, with the full accountability of the authorities to the people.

But in the spring of 1918 as well as in 1919, the situation was so different that Lenin had to change his views accordingly. He even thought it might be possible to go over to socialism and communism by abolishing trade and market; money relations; implementing direct exchange of goods and products and distribution; as well as nationalizing even petty industry, as an alternative to socializing key industries alone.

Lenin with Trotsky (centre) at a Red Square celebration of the second anniversary of the Revolution in 1919. The photograph emphasizes the latter's significant presence in the formative years of the Soviet Union. In subsequent Soviet publications, 'the unperson' of Trotsky was frequently blanked out from photographs.

Later on, in 1921–2, the development by Lenin of the New Economic Policy signalled civil peace in the country. Internally there was co-operation with the majority of petty producers and even part of the bourgeoisie. Externally there was co-existence and co-operation with the capitalist world (trade, foreign concessions, etc.). The ideas of one man had undergone radical evolution over a mere five years. The study of that process in history could be very useful for the present.

Also, it is important openly to show to the people the way in which socialist ideas had been implemented. This could form the basis for resolving the issue of a future model of socialism in the USSR, under today's conditions. This, undoubtedly, is a task of great complexity.

But if we do not analyse the realities objectively and realistically, our society may again fall into the drugged sleep it has slept for decades. It is not only lies that are damaging – half-truths are no better, because they involve half-measures and an inconsistency of decisions. This would create a new crisis.

Our country has at all times had honest and talented scholars, historians included, for whom the truth was the main target of life. Thus, after the 20th Congress and in the early 1960s there were studies of which Soviet historical science can be proud. Their authors were Adamov, Volobuyev, Burdzhalov, Tarnovsky and Gefter, to name but a few. These scholars were brave enough to defend the truth in the face of the inevitable retribution 'from above'.

Manuscripts were scattered and originals rejected out of hand by publishing houses. Scientists were demoted. Many were just collecting factual material knowing that there would be no opportunity to publish their findings. So, when you see new historical works today, it does not mean that historians have suddenly had their eyes opened. What it means is that there was previously no chance for a historian to publish the results of years of intense work. As soon as historians were given the chance they published.

Why then are elements of a deformed Soviet historical consciousness still being taught to those who will decide the fate of perestroika and the future of the country tomorrow?

This year, even secondary schools had to cancel graduation exams in Soviet history, which I believe was right, for it would be immoral to repeat the lies contained in the text books about 'enemies of the people' and so on.

The text books and teaching aids for all levels of education are still far from a genuinely scientific history. They are still permeated by dogmas inherited from Stalin's personality cult and the stagnation period under Brezhnev.

I think the first step is to give up the practice of having only one book of history, which thus turns into a Bible of sorts. There should be several good history books for school and university students.

Their quality has to be dependent primarily on their scientific levels, rather than claims to a single, inviolable historical truth. We have already seen instances when interpretations which are more advantageous have been substituted for historical truth.

This 1938 anti-Trotsky Stalinist cartoon attacks him and other 'Old Bolsheviks' for feeding at the trough of the 'Fatherland'.

But we need more than just several good text books. We need a package of measures to enlighten the people historically. Britain, West Germany and France have for 200 years been publishing fundamental studies of history, including archive documents and popular literature in parallel. So far we have nothing of the kind in the Soviet Union, so we have to start from scratch. We need mass-circulation journals – collections, memoirs and biographies. We should publish chronicles and collections of documents. I think we need a popular historical journal for young people.

And, of course, we should not allow what has happened to the memoirs of Marshal Georgi Zhukov, which were published while he was still alive and then corrected after his death.

The history of the party is inseparable from the history of Soviet society. Don't you think it is unwise to study CPSU?

This is a heritage of the Stalinist period. 'The Short Course of the History of the CPSU(b)' was a pure apology for the Stalin regime. Its gist is on the last page: we were building socialism, and in the course of it we came to be at loggerheads with the enemies of the people; we destroyed these enemies and built socialism.

This scheme was reproduced in full in the book of history edited by Boris Ponomaryov. Later editions of the book present the same formula, only a little diluted: this or that congress or plenum adopted this or that decision; the party mobilized the people to implementation of the decision; and it was implemented. The question of how it was done was presumably for another book of history!

But the history of the party is only a part of our whole history. Other issues present themselves. In the late 1970s and early 1980s Soviet society was in a deadlock. This was admitted by the April 1985 and January 1987 plenums of the Central Committee. In the course of the revolutionary transformation we are searching for a way out.

But since the party is the guiding force of our society, the people, quite naturally, are wondering how the party allowed society to enter the deadlock in the first place. Therefore, we need to know all stages of the development of the party. Logically, the history of the party should be studied as a part of our common history.

A book of history of the Communist Party of the Soviet Union is applicable to the higher party schools and at history faculties of universities. But I think in the end books of history will contain both the history of the party and society as a whole.

Archives are closely related to history. Not only specialists, but the public at large, are keen to have access to them today. What are your views?

Let me first say that archives are a measure of social consciousness and a reflection of socio-political problems. The composition of our archives helps to clarify the image of our society. Unfortunately, our archives have become appendices of the bureaucratic machine. We keep all sorts of official documents, all decrees, directives and decisions across the hierarchic ladder. You would not find any documents reflecting the everyday life of common people!

Accessibility is a measure of society's openness. So far the USSR has no law to regulate the term during which documents are considered classified, to be declassified after its expiry. We still cannot get free access to the documents of the 3rd (political) Department of the Tsarist Police. There are some classified documents dating back to the seventeenth century!

Party archives are also closed. The KGB, the Interior Ministry, the Foreign Ministry, the Defence Ministry and the State Committee for Statistics all have their own archives and regulations for access to them.

Lenin's idea of a single system of archives has not been realized. The explanation is simple. Both the party and the state apparatus have been bureaucratic. They have believed that secrecy is power.

*M*arshal Zhukov, hero of the Soviet Union and Stalin's
commander-in-chief in the Second World War. His memoirs were
'corrected' after his death in 1974.

So they have locked the doors to their archives and kept the keys.

Archives are being opened now. The chief of the USSR Institute of Archives, Vaganov, disclosed recently that over two million documents have been transferred to open archives. But what we want to know is the number of documents which are still classified.

Yet figures are not the essence of the matter. Take any resolution of the Central Committee. It says that this and this has been resolved and states the tasks that need to be carried out. But all accompanying materials (speeches and background materials) are closed. Millions of documents should not have been closed in the first place. As long as there is no corresponding law we will not set the archives right!

You are a member of the Soviet-American Cultural Initiative Foundation, sponsored by the American financier Soros. Will the initiatives apply to Soviet archives?

A certain sum of money will be spent for the implementation of an electronic archives programme. Our students will be involved in it. To begin with, we plan to deal with private archives in the USSR, of which there are many thousands.

Also, we are planning to deal with similar archives of our colleagues abroad. At the very least, we will compile a catalogue of these archives.

There is a plan to publish unpublished handwritten documents kept in private collections, more often than not with only a single copy. We are contemplating the creation of a special open-for-all fund to keep historical and other documents from private collections.

Speaking about our Institute, I should mention the Oral History Programme. Our students travel around the country recording their talks with veterans of the October Revolution, the Civil War, collectivization and industrialization, as well as the Second World War.

They collect testimonies of the repressed and survivors of the horrible famine of 1933. There is a lot of work which is more important for the USSR than any other country, for the people's memory has not so far been properly recorded.

We are now clearing up the blank spots of our history. The Commission on Rehabilitation is rehabilitating many names of eminent party and state officials. Yet has the historical truth been completely restored?

I think it is abnormal that biographies of Kamenev, Zinoviev, Bukharin and others who at one time stood at the helm of the party and the state were written only by foreign historians. This is explained partly by the twenty-year interruption in the rehabilitation of Stalin's victims.

Perestroika is in full swing, yet we do not have a single fully-fledged biography of all the people surrounding Lenin, written by a Soviet historian. These documents too are closed. Without them we will not be able to fill in all the blank spots.

I believe we should again publish books by Milyukov, Kerensky, Denikin, Kolchak and other eminent figures of Soviet history, whatever their political orientation. This was actually done in the 1920s. A scientific approach means an unbiased inclusion in our assessment of all the main figures and their actual words and deeds.

Now what we used to do, i.e. introduce chosen people and some of their ideas, is faking history. Meanwhile, we are still publishing books like *Near the Kremlin Wall* which presents Stalin and his henchmen in a rosy light. We must have objective, scientific biographies of the key people in our history.

I have spoken of what have become known as the blank spots of Soviet history, but have not yet covered the largest blank spot, that of Leon Trotsky. Until we write an unbiased and scientific biography of this man, we will have difficulties in restoring the historical truth.

Stalin's version of Trotsky is unacceptable, for it is false throughout. I have no personal sympathy for Trotsky, but I do believe he deserves a truthful analysis. Trotsky, for one thing, played a very positive role in the October Revolution, during the Civil War and the restoration of the economy.

This corresponds to Lenin's assessment of the man. Nor should we overlook Trotsky's active criticism of Stalin and Stalinism when he was in the Soviet Union and then abroad. Also, it is being admitted now that Stalin was implementing many of Trotsky's ideas. However, I do not think this is very accurate, since what is meant here is Trotsky's heritage of the Civil War period, of war communism and even earlier.

There is another side to the coin. A. Kuzmin, who writes for *Nash Sovremennik* (Our Contemporary), wrote recently that Trotsky was 'Euro-centric', a phenomenon alien to the Soviet Union. But this casts a shadow on the Bolshevik Party, for Trotsky was one of its leaders. Incidentally, Kuzmin never brings his idea to a logical conclusion, just substituting Bolshevism for Trotskyism. This highlights the need for an objective biography of Leon Trotsky.

Our historical literature is very unreliable concerning inner-party struggle, limited as it is to half-truths at best. Perestroika and a scientific assessment of history are greatly interdependent. Admittedly, the path we are following is no bed of roses.

But we had to have no doubts when stepping on this path. It is only historical studies devoid of all sorts of ideological dogmas that are capable of comprehending our past, and restoring our social identity. This has to be a prerequisite of every society.

Translated by Vladimir Voronin and Adam Shulman.

Further Reading

CHAPTER I
The Idea of Holy Russia

G.P. Fedotov, *The Russian Religious Mind*, 2 vols. (Harvard University Press, 1966); G. Florovsky and others, 'The Problem of Old Russian Culture,' *Slavic Review*, vols. 21, 22 (1962-3); J. Meyendorff, *Byzantium and the Rise of Russia* (Cambridge University Press, 1981); D. Obolensky, *Byzantium and the Slavs: Collected Studies* (Variorum, 1971).

CHAPTER II
The West comes to Russian Architecture

G.H. Hamilton, *The Art and Architecture of Russia*, 3rd edn. (Penguin Books, 1983); M. Alpatov, *Russian Impact on Art* (Greenwood, 1950); *An Introduction to Russian Art and Architecture*, eds. R. Auty and D. Oblensky (Cambridge University Press, 1980); William Brumfield, *Gold in Azure. One Thousand Years of Russian Architecture* (David R. Godine, Boston, 1983); James Cracraft, *The Petrine Revolution in Russian Architecture* (University of Chicago Press, 1988); L.A.J. Hughes, 'The 17th-century "Renaissance" in Russia' (*History Today*, February, 1980), and 'Russia's first architectural books: a chapter in Peter the Great's cultural revolution' (*Architectural Design*, 53, nos. 5/6, 1983).

CHAPTER III
European Images of Muscovy

The analysis here is based upon the English translation of Herberstein: *Notes on Russia*, ed. R.H. Major, 2 vols. (London, 1851–2). The introduction includes useful biographical and bibliographical material; Giles Fletcher, *Of the Russe Commonwealth*, eds. Richard Pipes and John V.A. Fine Jr (Harvard University Press, 1966); T.S. Willan, *The Early History of the Russia Company 1553–1603* (University of Manchester Press, 1956); Samuel H. Baron, trans. and ed., *The Travels of Olearius in Seventeenth-Century Russia* (Stanford University Press, 1967).

CHAPTER IV
Tsar Alexis goes to War

Philip Longworth's chapter in *Absolutism in Seventeenth-Century Europe*, ed. J. Miller (Macmillan Press, 1990); Philip Longworth, *Alexis. Tsar of All the*

Russias (Secker and Warburg, 1984). For some general background consult George Vernadsky, *The Tsardom of Moscow 1547–1682*, (Part 2, Yale University Press, 1969, vol. V, Part 2 of his *A History of Russia*) or V.O. Klyuchevsky, *The Rise of the Romanovs* (Macmillan, 1970).

CHAPTER V
Muscovy looks West

The present article is based on my research and interpretation set forth in greater detail in *The Well Ordered Police State – Social and Institutional Change through Law in the Germanies and Russia, 1600–1800* (Yale University Press, 1983) and *Understanding Imperial Russia – State and Society in the Old Regime* (Columbia University Press, 1984). There is no adequate study of the reign of Peter I in English, the most readable is V.O. Klyuchevsky, *Peter the Great* (Vintage Books, 1961). Detailed information on seventeenth-century Muscovy can be found in George Vernadsky, *The Tsardom of Moscow, 1547–1682* (Yale University Press, 1969). For a stimulating and controversial interpretation of modern Russian history as a whole, see Richard Pipes, *Russia under the Old Regime* (Weidenfeld and Nicolson, 1974). There is also Lindsey Hughes, *Sophia, Regent of Russia 1657-1704* (Yale University Press, 1990); Ivan Pososhkov, *The Book of Poverty and Wealth*, ed. and trans. A.P. Vlasto and L.R. Lewitter (The Athlone Press, 1987).

CHAPTER VI
Russia's Rise as a European Power

Paul Dukes, *The Making of Russian Absolutism 1613–1801* (Longman, 1982); Philip Longworth, *Alexis. Tsar of all the Russias* (Secker and Warburg, 1984); M.S. Anderson, *Peter the Great* (Thames and Hudson, 1978); Norman Davies, *God's Playground. A History of Poland* vol. I (Oxford University Press, 1981); Ragnhild Hatton, *Charles XII of Sweden* (Weidenfeld and Nicolson, 1968); Christopher Duffy, *Russia's Military Way to the West* (Routledge and Kegan Paul, 1981); B.H. Summer, *Peter the Great and the Ottoman Empire* (Oxford University Press, 1949); Lindsey Hughes, *Sophia. Regent of Russia 1657-1704* (Yale University Press, 1990); M. Roberts, *From Oxenstierna to Charles XII* (Cambridge University Press, 1991); J. Black, *The Rise of the European Powers 1679-1793* (Edward Arnold, 1990); J. Black, *Eighteenth Century Europe* (Macmillan, 1990); J. Black, *A Military Revolution? Military Change and European Society* (Macmillan, 1991); O. Subtelny, *Domination of Eastern Europe. Native Nobilities and Foreign Absolutism 1500-1715* (Alan Sutton, 1986); J. Lukowski, *Liberty's Folly. The Polish-Lithuanian Commonwealth in the Eighteenth Century* (Routledge, 1991); G. Barany, *The Anglo-Russian Entente Cordiale of 1697-1698* (Columbia University Press, 1986).

CHAPTER VII
On Crime and Punishment

The most useful collection of foreigners' accounts of sixteenth-century Russia is *Rude and Barbarous Kingdom*, eds. Lloyd E. Berry and Robert O. Crummey

(University of Wisconsin Press, 1968). In English the only systematic life of Peter Tolstoi is in Nikolai Tolstoy, *The Tolstoys* (Hamish Hamilton, 1983); see also my translation of the diary, Max J. Okenfuss, *The Travel Diary of Peter Tolstoi. A Muscovite in Early Modern Europe* (Northern Illinois University Press, 1987). Efforts to transform the Russian clergy can be traced in James Cracraft, *The Church Reform of Peter the Great* (Stanford University Press, 1971), and Gregory L. Freeze, *The Russian Levites* (Harvard University Press, 1977). The distinction between Leonine and Cyrillian Christianity was developed by G.P. Fedotov, *The Russian Religious Mind. Kievan Christianity: the 10th to the 13th Centuries* (Harper, 1960), and the turn to Protestantism is best read in Georges Florovsky, *Ways of Russian Theology*, Part 1 (Nordland, 1979).

CHAPTER VIII
Peter the Great and the Modern World

Valentin Boss, *Newton and Russia: the early influence 1698–1796* (Oxford University Press, 1972); Paul Hazard, *The European Mind 1680–1715* (Penguin Books, 1973); *Peter the Great transforms Russia* ed. James Cracraft (Heath & Co., 1991); Adriano Tilgher, *Homo Faber*, translated as *Work, what it has meant to men through the ages* by D.C. Fisher (London, 1931); Arthur M. Wilson, 'The "philosophes" in the light of present day theories of modernisation', *Studies on Voltaire in the Eighteenth Century*, ed. Theodore Besterman, vol. LVIII, (1967).

CHAPTER IX
Klyuchevsky and the Course of Russian History

There is an item on Klyuchevsky by A. Parry in *Some Historians of Modern Europe*, ed. B.E. Schmitt (Kennikat Publishers, Port Washington, 1966); A.G. Mazour, 'V.O. Klyuchevsky, The Making of a Historian' (*Russian Review*, 31, 1972); N.V. Riasanovsky, 'Kliuchevskii, Vasilii Osipovich', *the Modern Encyclopedia of Russian and Soviet History*, vol. 49 (1988); V.O. Klyuchevsky, *Peter the Great*, trans. L. Archibald (Macmillan, 1958); *The Rise of the Romanovs*, trans. L. Archibald (Macmillan, 1970); guest ed. Marc Raeff, *Kliuchevsky's Russia: Critical Studies, Canadian American Slavic Studies*, 20th Anniversary vol., part 2 (1986).

CHAPTER X
Hrushevsky and the Ukraine's 'Lost' History

None of Hrushevsky's scholarly works has been translated into English, but his survey *History of Ukraine* (Yale University Press, 1941) and *Historical Evolution of the Ukrainian Problem* (reprinted John T. Zubal, 1981) give a glimpse of his approach and style. Thomas Prymak, *Mykhailo Hrushevsky: The Politics of National Culture* (University of Toronto Press, 1987); N. Polonska-Vasylenko, *Two Conceptions of the History of Ukraine and Russia* (Association of Ukrainians in Great Britain, 1968); Lubomyr Wynar, *Mykhailo Hrushevsky: Ukrainian-Russian Confrontation in Historiography* (Ukrainian Historical Association, 1988).

List of contributors

PAUL DUKES is Professor of History and Director of the Centre for Soviet and East European Studies at the University of Aberdeen. He is the author of *A History of Europe* (1985), *The Last Great Game: USA versus USSR* (1989); *The Making of Russian Absolutism* (2nd ed., 1990); *A History of Russia* (2nd ed., 1990).

SERGEI AVERINTSEV is Professor of Classical Philology at Moscow University, a Member of the Academy of Sciences and the author of *From Bosphorus to Euphrates: Poetry and Religion in the First Christian Millennium* (1987).

LINDSEY HUGHES is Senior Lecturer in Russian History at the School of Slavonic and East European Studies, University of London, where she specializes in teaching Medieval and Early Modern Russian history and the history of Russian art. Her books include *Russia and the West: Prince Vasily Vasil'evich Golitsyn (1643–1714)* (1984) and *Sophia Regent of Russia 1657–1704* (1990). She is currently working on a book on Russia in the reign of Peter the Great.

SAMUEL BARON is Professor of History at the University of North Carolina, and author of *Muscovite Russia: Collected Essays* (1980) and *Explorations in Muscovite History* (1991).

PHILIP LONGWORTH is Professor of History at McGill University, Canada. He is author of *Alexis, Tsar of All the Russias* (1984) and a contributor to *Absolutism in Seventeenth Century Europe*, ed. J. Miller (1990).

MARC RAEFF is Bakhmeteff Professor Emeritus of Russian Studies at Columbia University, New York. He is the author of *Michael Speransky, Statesman of Imperial Russia 1772–1839* (1969); *The Well Ordered Police State – Social and Institutional Change through Law in the Germanies and Russia, 1600–1800* (1983); *Understanding Imperial Russia – State and Society in the Old Regime* (1984); and *Russia Abroad – A Cultural History of the Russian Emigration 1919–1939* (1990).

JEREMY BLACK is Director of the Research Foundation and Society of Fellows of Durham University and Senior Lecturer in History. His twelve books include *Eighteenth Century Europe* (1990), *A Military Revolution?* (1991) and *The Rise of the European Powers* (1990).

MAX J. OKENFUSS is Associate Professor of History at Washington University, St. Louis. He is the author of many articles on early-modern Russian education and *The Discovery of Childhood in Russia: The Evidence of the Slavic Primer* (1980), and the translator of *The Travel Diary of Peter Tolstoi* (1987); he is also the American editor of the *Jahrbücher für Geschichte Osteuropas*, and has just completed a study of Russia's reaction to the Latinate culture of the West, 1648–1789.

L.R. LEWITTER is a Fellow of Christ's College and Professor Emeritus of Slavonic Studies at the University of Cambridge, and co-editor of *The Book of Poverty and Wealth, 1724* (1985).

THOMAS M. PRYMAK is Assistant Professor of History and Canada Research Fellow at McMaster University, Hamilton, Canada. He has written widely on Russian and East European history and on the history of the Slavic communities in North America. His study of Michael Hrushevsky won the Ukrainian Historical Association Prize for 1985.

YURI AFANASYEV is Rector of the Moscow Archive Institute.

Illustration Acknowledgements

Society for Cultural Relations with the USSR cover; Mansell Collection 11; Mansell/ Alinari 14; Biblioteca Apostolica Vaticana 17; Mansell Collection 21; Novosti Press Agency 25, 28; Lindsey Hughes 31, 33; History Today Archives 37, 39, 40; from Giles Fletcher, *Of the Russe Commonwealth* (1591) 44; History Today Archives 47; Novosti Press Agency 49; Central State Archives of Ancient Arts, Moscow 51; History Today Archives 54, 57, 60; Novosti Press Agency 62; History Today Archives 65; Novosti Press Agency 67; History Today Archives 68; Novosti Press Agency 70, 73, 77; History Today Archives 78; Novosti Press Agency 80, 81; History Today Archives 85, 86; Novosti Press Agency 89; by gracious permission of Her Majesty the Queen 93; by permission of the Earl of Crawford and Balcarres 99; History Today Archives 102; Novosti Press Agency 106; Paul Dukes 109; Mansell Collection 111, 113, 114; Thomas Prymak 117; History Today Archives 119; Society for Cultural Relations with the USSR 120; History Today Archives 122; Hulton Picture Company 125; David King Collection 128-9, 131, 133.

Index

Numbers in **bold** refer to illustrations